W9-BWD-582

Trauma-Sensitive Schools

WITHDRAWN

SAGINAW CHIPPEWA ACADEMY
LIBRARY MEDIA CENTER
MT. PLEASANT, MI 48858

SAGINAW CHIPPEWA ACADEMY
LIBRARY MEDIA CENTER
MT. PLEASANT, MI 48858

Trauma-Sensitive Schools

Learning Communities
Transforming Children's Lives, K–5

Susan E. Craig

Jane Ellen Stevens
FOREWORD

TEACHERS COLLEGE PRESS

TEACHERS COLLEGE | COLUMBIA UNIVERSITY
NEW YORK AND LONDON

Published by Teachers College Press, 1234 Amsterdam Avenue, New York, NY 10027

Copyright © 2016 by Teachers College, Columbia University

Foreword © by Jane Ellen Stevens

All rights reserved. No part of this publication may be reproduced or transmitted in any form or by any means, electronic or mechanical, including photocopy, or any information storage and retrieval system, without permission from the publisher.

Figure 2.2, Revised ACE Pyramid, courtesy of Vincent Felitti. Used with permission.

Appendix A, Resources for Professional Development, courtesy of Jane Ellen Stevens. Used with permission.

Library of Congress Cataloging-in-Publication Data

Names: Craig, Susan E., author.
Title: Trauma-sensitive schools : learning communities transforming
   children's lives, K-5 / Susan E. Craig.
Description: New York, NY : Teachers College Press, [2016] | Includes
   bibliographical references and index.
Identifiers: LCCN 2015030891 | ISBN 9780807757451 (pbk.) | ISBN 9780807774533
   (ebook)
Subjects: LCSH: Problem children—Education (Early childhood) | Problem
   children—Behavior modification. | Psychic trauma in children. |
   Post-traumatic stress disorder in children. | Stress in children. |
   Learning, Psychology of. | Educational psychology. | Affective education.
   | Community and school. | Teacher-student relationships.
Classification: LCC LC4801 .C599 2015 | DDC 372.21—dc23
LC record available at http://lccn.loc.gov/2015030891

ISBN 978-0-8077-5745-1 (paper)
ISBN 978-0-8077-7453-3 (ebook)

Printed on acid-free paper
Manufactured in the United States of America

23 22 21 20 19 18 17   8 7 6 5

Contents

Foreword

A sea change is coursing slowly but resolutely through this nation's education system. Tens of thousands of schools have discarded—or are discarding—a highly punitive approach to school discipline in favor of schools that are supportive and compassionate.

The formula is simple, really: Instead of waiting for kids to behave badly and then punishing them, schools are creating environments in which kids can succeed. The secret to success doesn't involve the kids so much as it does the adults: Focus on changing how teachers and administrators interact with children and, almost like magic, the kids stop fighting, acting out, or withdrawing in class. They're more interested in school, they're happier, and they feel safer.

It was in 1995 that our education system lost its way. Just one year after the U.S. Congress passed the Gun-Free Schools Act of 1994, the adoption of broad zero-tolerance policies spread like a prairie fire to schools across the United States. Once zero tolerance was locked in, teachers and principals warped it, some say, by the pressure to perform well on tests. Kick the troublemakers out, and there's less disruption and interruption in class. With those underperforming kids gone, test scores look better.

Suspensions and expulsions soared to ridiculous levels. By 2007, a stunning one-quarter of all public high school students had been suspended at least once during their school careers, according to a National Center for Education Statistics 2011 report. The numbers were worse for boys of color. One-third of Hispanic boys and 57% of black boys had been kicked out of school at least once (NCES, 2011).

Here's the absurd part: Only 5% of these suspensions or expulsions were for weapons or drugs. The other 95%? "Disruptive behavior" and "other." This includes cell phone use, violation of dress code, talking back to a teacher, bringing scissors to class for an art project, giving Midol to a classmate, and, in at least one case, farting.

But punishment doesn't change behavior; it just drops hundreds of thousands of kids into a school-to-prison pipeline. The cost to taxpayers is $292,000 per dropout over her or his lifetime due to costs for more po-lice, courts, and prisons, plus loss of income and taxes ("Dropout Nation," 2012). The shift from a punitive to a supportive approach has come from two different sources: (1) From educators who were teaching children with behavior disorders, or who were creating programs to help kids deal with violence (particularly shootings) in and around their schools. (2) From those who were adapting restorative justice practices developed for the criminal justice system. All methods focused on the social and emotional lives of children, such as teaching children respect, empathy, and coping skills. Equipped with their own conflict resolution skills, teachers could defuse most situations in their classrooms instead of sending disruptive kids to the principal's office.

The methods now have names such as PBIS (Positive Behavioral Inter-vention and Support), Safe & Civil Schools, CBITS (Cognitive Behavioral Intervention for Trauma in Schools), and restorative justice.

But a perfect storm of research shows that those methods don't go far enough. This new research—which is also beginning to revolutionize prac-tices in the areas of mental health, substance abuse, social services, youth services, pediatrics, and juvenile justice systems—has been called the unified science, or "theory of everything," of human development. It combines the CDC-Kaiser Permanente Adverse Childhood Experiences Study (see http://www.cdc.gov/violenceprevention/acestudy/), the neurobiology of toxic stress, the long-term biomedical and epigenetic consequences of toxic stress, and resilience research (Nakazawa, 2015).

In a nutshell, this research shows that the toxic stress of trauma can damage children's brains, making it impossible for them to learn; punitive school discipline policies just further traumatize them. The research also pokes big, ragged holes in the long-held belief that if a child who's failing just works harder, she or he will achieve success.

Susan Craig's book, *Trauma-Sensitive Schools*, couldn't have come at a better time. In the book, she points out that this research is essential knowl-edge if educators want to create a school system where all children can feel safe enough to learn and succeed academically.

As Craig writes: "Until schools acknowledge the seriousness of this problem and commit to resolving it, the failure of other educational reform initiatives will continue. Trauma is not just a mental health problem. It is an educational problem that, left unaddressed, derails the academic achieve-ment of thousands of children."

In trauma-sensitive schools, however, resilience-building practices can soothe those kids and turn them back into the happy learning engines that they are in their healthy and natural states. In trauma-sensitive schools, teachers are happier, less stressed, and better at their jobs.

The trauma-sensitive—also called trauma-informed—schools movement is less than a decade old. As with any good idea whose time has come, its beginnings occurred in many parts of the country, including Washington State, Massachusetts, California, and New York City.

What makes trauma-sensitive schools so important is that they don't just address the kids who are acting out. The teachers and administrators in these schools understand that the basic reaction to trauma is not just fight, but is also flight or fright (i.e., freeze). So they make sure that they're also helping the kids who tune out, who fall asleep in class, or who isolate themselves in the classroom, in the cafeteria, or on the playground. These are the kids who aren't at risk of being kicked out of school—these are the kids who drop out of education altogether.

Specifically, this book will help teachers and administrators create a trauma-sensitive school that

- stops traumatizing already traumatized children;
- helps not only traumatized students who express their trauma by acting out, but also those who withdraw;
- and creates socially and emotionally safe environments where children can learn, teachers can teach, and administrators can manage successful schools.

Trauma-Sensitive Schools comes at a critical time for education. After Washington State did its own statewide survey of the prevalence of adverse childhood experiences, it calculated that in a public school classroom of 30 students, more than half were exposed to physical abuse or adult-on-adult violence in their homes or neighborhoods (Anda & Brown, 2010). This is not unique to Washington State; because of the prevalence of childhood adversity, you can find the same issues in any state and city in the United States. Imagine what those kids bring to school with them, and how their behavior affects those around them. Teachers don't have to imagine it; they see it every single day.

Jane Ellen Stevens
Founder and Publisher
ACEs Connection Network

REFERENCES

Anda, R. F., & Brown, D. W. (2010). *Adverse childhood experiences and population health in Washington.* Retrieved from http://www.legis.state.wv.us/senate1/majority/poverty/ACEsinWashington2009BRFSSFinalReport%20-%20Crittenton.pdf

Dropout Nation. (2012). Retrieved from http://www.pbs.org/wgbh/pages/frontline/education/dropout-nation/by-the-numbers-dropping-out-of-high-school/

Nakazawa, D. J. (2015). *Childhood disrupted: How your biography becomes your biology, and how you can heal.* New York, NY: Atria Books.

National Center for Education Statistics (NCES) (2011). Retrieved from http://nces.ed.gov/pubs2012/2012026/tables/table_14.asp

Introduction

My interest in understanding the relationship between violence and children's cognitive development began in the early 1980s when I was working as a reading teacher. I wanted to know why so many young, aggressive children, who did not meet the criteria for learning disabilities or developmental delay, were unable to read. The question led me to doctoral studies at the University of New Hampshire's Family Research Lab, where I completed a dissertation on the effects of violence on children's cognitive development. The results showed a relationship between exposure to family violence and deficits in children's language development, memory, attention, and locus of control. Concerns about the causal direction of the relationships tempered the power of these findings.

Disagreements about causality were still an issue in 1992 when I published the article "The Educational Needs of Children Living in Violence" in *Phi Delta Kappan* (Craig, 1992). Some argued that abuse and neglect caused the observed developmental anomalies (Money, 1982). Others favored the view that children with developmental disabilities were more difficult to nurture, thus increasing their risk of maltreatment (Martin, 1979).

Since then, the retrospective Adverse Childhood Experiences (ACE) study (Felitti, Anda, Nordenberg, Williamson, Spitz, Edwards, & Marks, 1998) as well as research on children's neurological development (National Scientific Center on the Developing Child, 2005, 2006, 2007, 2012) have resolved these issues. There is no longer any doubt that violence and chronic exposure to toxic stress disrupt the process of normal child development (Perkins & Graham-Bermann, 2012). These experiences alter the architecture of children's brains in ways that threaten their ability to achieve academic and social competence. Left unattended, these can affect health and well-being not only of children, but adults as well (Karr-Morse & Wiley, 2012). But the news is not all bad. Brain development turns out to be a very dynamic process that retains a certain plasticity or capacity to adapt throughout the human life span. This ability to change offers hope that the effects of early trauma can be reversed later in life (National Child Traumatic Stress Network, 2009). With the right type of instruction and emotional support, traumatized children can regain their ability to achieve academic and social mastery.

Regrettably, these new advances in neuroscience are not yet center stage in discussions of educational reform. Despite its availability since the 1990s, this research does not inform the nation's educational policies, nor is it discussed in educational journals or publications (Oehlberg, 2012). Very few school districts or teachers' colleges provide information about the effects of trauma on brain development, the implications for school achievement, and proven ways to compensate for the developmental problems trauma creates for young children.

POSSIBLE REASONS FOR THE DISCONNECT

One reason for this apparent disconnect may be what is referred to as the "silo effect," which occurs when institutional system components stay within their own area of specialization and fail to communicate with each other (Ensor, 1988). A good example of this in the field of education is the lack of contact and communication among curriculum specialists and assessment specialists, and K–5 teachers and middle school teachers.

In some cases the silo effect is so extreme that the inhabitants of one silo do not even see the other silos. The results are thwarted communication, wasted energy, and missed opportunities for information exchange and shared policy development. Good examples are when teachers fail to pass along accommodations or adaptive equipment children with disabilities may need to complete written assignments. Another example is when strategies that are effective in helping a child with low frustration tolerance remain calm in new or challenging situations are not communicated to other professionals working with the child.

The silo effect is a possible explanation for some of the failure of education reform efforts since the turn of the 21st century. With the passage of No Child Left Behind (NCLB, 2001), reform efforts focused on standards and test-based accountability (Zhao, 2014). *Race to the Top* promises systemic reform by raising standards and improving teacher effectiveness. While laudable, neither effort includes research or information developed outside the educational framework. Specifically, neither is influenced by the wealth of neuroscience research currently available on the developing brain and its effects on children's learning and behavior (Caine & Caine, 1990; Jensen, 2008; Willis, 2008). Nor do they address the readily available explanations of the relationship between childhood adversity, neural development, and academic achievement.

Trauma-Sensitive Schools: Learning Communities Transforming Children's Lives K–5 attempts to spark a dialogue between members of the educational and neuroscience silos. Equipped with the knowledge produced by a multidisciplinary approach, policymakers can view educational reform through a trauma-sensitive lens: one that recognizes the high cost of trauma, as well as the pervasiveness of its symptoms, and that promotes resiliency as an antidote to failure.

DESIGN OF THE BOOK

Chapter 1, Trauma-Sensitive Schools: A Resource for School Improvement, traces the history of the trauma-sensitive school movement. The assumptions of a trauma-sensitive approach are discussed, as well as the model's core components. Implications of the implementation of this approach for educational reform are reviewed.

Chapter 2, Dealing with Student Trauma: A Missing Component of Educational Reform, provides a review of the research that established a causal relationship between early childhood trauma and the subsequent pattern of developmental deficits that threatens children's academic and social success. The chapter explains how these occur as the result of changes in brain architecture caused by trauma and related attachment failures. It concludes with an introduction to the trauma-sensitive school movement, thought by many to be the best way to improve children's academic and social success.

Chapter 3, The Neurology of Attachment: Caregiving Counts, discusses the social nature of the brain, addressing how early experiences shape children's ability to form and sustain relationships. It explains how the attachment bond is the carrier of all development, responsible for children's self-definition and their perception of others. Readers are introduced to strategies to engage traumatized children, thereby avoiding painful cycles of reenactment or oppositional behavior. The chapter concludes with a discussion of how positive attachment relationships at school help children gain the courage they need to move beyond the paralyzing effects of early trauma.

Chapter 4, Trauma's Effects on Children's Readiness to Learn, provides a detailed explanation of the impact of early trauma on children's academic and social competence. Changes in brain organization and function are discussed in terms of how they affect the development of children's representational thought, language, memory, attention, and executive function. Recommendations about how to help children overcome these obstacles are provided.

Chapter 5, Retooling the Teacher's Role in Trauma-Sensitive Schools, begins with a discussion of children's neurodevelopment and instructional best practices. The benefits of differentiated instruction and dialogic teaching are reviewed, including the contribution each makes to children's developing sense of efficacy and self-awareness. A system of tiered intervention is proposed as well as strategies teachers can use to create collaborative partnerships with students.

Chapter 6, Nature's Second Chance: Constructing a Reflective Brain, introduces the reader to recommended instructional strategies that positively affect the development of the cortical areas of the brain. Emphasis is placed on practices that promote self-reflection, mindfulness, and systemic integration of new information. Each practice strengthens the neural pathways responsible for self-regulation, a fundamental area of concern in children with early trauma histories.

Chapter 7, Recognizing the Emotional Work of Teachers, explores the emotional toll of working with traumatized children and its possible relationship to teacher attrition. The need for training that informs teachers about the contagious nature of trauma is discussed as well as ways to promote teacher resilience.

Chapter 8, Next Steps—Managing the Necessary Changes to School Policies and Practices, provides an overview of steps to consider as schools adopt a trauma-sensitive approach. These include an awareness of the complexity of the proposed changes, as well as the resources required to sustain enthusiasm and support for the process. The role of district and local leadership is discussed, in addition to the need for progress monitoring and the evaluation of student outcomes.

CONCLUSION

While one book cannot resolve all of the issues related to trauma and learning, it can raise awareness of a problem that threatens the viability of a valued resource—America's public schools. The path to true school reform requires educators to embrace the insights neuroscience provides into this troubling barrier to children's academic and social competence. The goal of writing *Trauma-Sensitive Schools: Learning Communities Transforming Children's Lives K–5* is to provide educators with guidance along the way.

CHAPTER 1

Trauma-Sensitive Schools

A Resource for School Improvement

> What cannot be talked about can also not be put to rest . . . the wounds continue to fester from generation to generation.
>
> *—Bruno Bettelheim*

Trauma-sensitive schools emphasize safety, empowerment, and collaborative partnerships between children and adults. Within this model children's negative behaviors are the direct or indirect result of an "injury" caused by physical, emotional, or social maltreatment.

This chapter discusses the failure of "one size fits all" student discipline, particularly in relationship to children with early trauma histories. Research that establishes a link between trauma and children's academic and social failures provides educators with a new paradigm for interpreting students' misbehavior. Once educators understand the assumptions and core components of trauma-sensitive service delivery, decisions can be made about the best way to integrate them into all aspects of the school day.

THE IMPORTANCE OF THE TRAUMA-SENSITIVE SCHOOLS MOVEMENT

The trauma-sensitive schools movement is the result of a confluence of forces that are changing the paradigm through which educators view children's academic and social problems:

- The failure of "zero-tolerance" policies to resolve the issues of school safety, bullying, and academic failure that continue to plague many schools
- Growing evidence that supports the relationship between early trauma and academic failure (Annie E. Casey Foundation, 2013;

5

Institute of Medicine of the National Academies, 2013; Perkins & Graham-Bermann, 2012)

- A new understanding of children's disruptive behavior and how best to extinguish it (Perry, 2013)

Together these forces represent a new vision for promoting children's success—the vision of a trauma-sensitive school.

Failure of Zero-Tolerance Policies

In the years following the Columbine High School shootings in 1999, schools embraced zero-tolerance discipline policies aimed at controlling school violence. These policies impose severe penalties on children without regard for individual circumstances, and often blur the boundaries between school and police authority. As a result, many schools now rely on law enforcement to handle minor misconduct (Elais, 2013).

Rather than improving school safety, zero-tolerance policies put children at increased risk of arrest for being tardy, having a temper tantrum, or disturbing the peace. In many states, there is a growing tendency to view prison as the default educational placement for children whose behavior is deemed unruly or out of control.

Children of color and those with emotional disabilities are disproportionately represented in this so-called school to prison pipeline (Quinn, Rutherford, & Leone, 2001; Snyder, 2005). Despite efforts on the part of the American Bar Association (ABA Juvenile Justice, Zero Tolerance Policy Report, 2001), civil rights organizations (Elais, 2013), and United States Senator Dick Durbin (Dianis, 2012), zero-tolerance policies remain an ongoing threat to children's ability to access a free and appropriate public school education. Trauma-sensitive schools offer an alternative to this type of coercive discipline.

Growing Evidence That Links Trauma and Academic Failure

Although some traumatized children do well in school, the majority do not (Craig, 1992; Groves, 2002; Osofsky & Osofsky, 1999). Their difficulty in meeting the academic and social challenges of school appear related to behaviors that are dysregulated or out of control and to trouble acquiring basic skills such as reading proficiency (Annie E. Casey Foundation, 2013; De Bellis, 2006).

Frequent absences, or time away from class due to disruptive behaviors, result in lost instructional time, which in turn causes gaps in children's knowledge of core curriculum. Deficits in executive skills make organizing materials and meeting deadlines difficult, while a disproportionately high level of problematic peer relationships limits their capacity for collaborative small group work (Institute of Medicine of the National Academies, 2013).

As a result, traumatized children have lower scores on standardized tests (Cook, Spinazzola, Lanktree, Blaustein, Sprague, Cloitre, 2007), higher referrals to special education (Jonson-Reid, Drake, Kim, Porterfield, & Han, 2004), higher dropout rates (Porche, Fortuna, Lin, & Alegria, 2011), and are more likely than peers to engage in delinquent behavior (Lansford, Miller-Johnson, Berlin, Dodge, Bates, & Pettit, 2007).

Insights from Neuroscience

Neuroscientists now agree that the brain is a social organ. It develops within the context of attachment relationships, which either ensure its health or threaten its survival. There are now thousands of studies that provide insight into how relationships influence neuroplasticity, or the brain's capacity to change, and learning (Cozolino, 2013). Together they signal a paradigm shift in how educators view children's disruptive behavior, and the role school experiences play in extinguishing it.

Understanding Disruptive Behaviors. Traditional explanations of children's disruptive behaviors often emphasize their volitional aspects, suggesting that they occur as a result of bad choices, or intentional defiance. Recommended interventions are contingency based, suggesting that all children will work for the right reward or to avoid unpleasant consequences. The inability of these techniques to effect the desired changes in children's behavior leaves many teachers struggling to understand why.

Recent studies of trauma and self-regulation provide an explanation. Throughout life the interpretation of danger involves a dialogue between the subcortical brain, immediately below the cerebral cortex, and the more sophisticated cortex. The cerebral cortex is the site of consciousness and higher-order thinking. It is the outer layer of the brain and is made up of folded gray matter (see Figure 1.1).

Early trauma limits children's ability to use higher-order thinking to regulate subcortical brain activity. Their thinking is "held hostage" by relentless fear and hyperarousal. These sensations cannot be contained or extinguished through traditional methods. Instead, interventions directed at regulating brain stem activity are required (Perry, 2013). Patterned rhythmic activities like walking, dancing, singing, and meditative breathing allow a

Figure 1.1. Diagram of the Human Brain

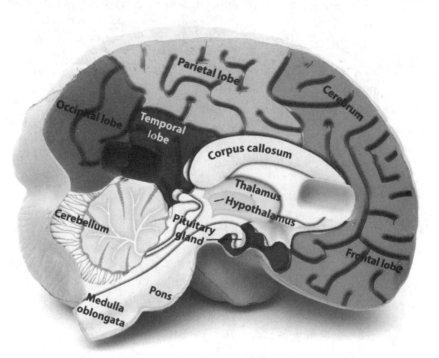

return to a calmer cognitive state, where problem solving and higher-order thinking can occur (Wiley, 2004).

Strengthening Neural Pathways. Helping children relax and be open to learning is an important first step in using school experience to reverse the damage inflicted by trauma. A comfortable level of arousal allows children to engage in learning activities that work with the brain's plasticity to strengthen the cortical areas of the brain affected by early trauma. These include executive skills, language, and impulse control (Perkins & Graham-Bermann, 2012).

The instructional strategies most beneficial to traumatized children are those that reinforce core concepts, scaffold new information on prior knowledge, use classroom discourse purposefully, and provide direct instruction in peer collaboration. When practiced consistently, these interventions help children use their brains advantageously to move beyond the limits imposed by their traumatic past.

RESPONDING TO THE HIGH PREVALENCE OF CHILDHOOD TRAUMA

Despite concerted efforts to effect reform, public schools continue to struggle. Many reasons are given for the demise of this once respected institution, including poor teacher performance (New America Foundation, 2013), student economic disparity (Duncan & Murnane, 2011), and the apparent disconnect between traditional instruction and the demanding social and economic environment of the 21st century (Cozolino, 2013).

What is ignored is the high prevalence of unresolved trauma among the student population (Oehlberg, 2012). In 2005, Massachusetts Advocates for Children (Cole, O'Brien, Gadd, Ristuccia, Wallace, & Gregory, 2005) broke the silence that surrounds this public health epidemic and introduced a framework for mitigating its effects.

The term *trauma-sensitive schools* was coined to describe the school climate, instructional designs, positive behavioral supports, and policies traumatized students need to achieve academic and social competence. Since then, California, Pennsylvania, Massachusetts, Washington, and Wisconsin are among the states leading the effort to draw national attention to the prevalence of trauma among school-aged children and the need to include the creation of trauma-sensitive environments in future reform efforts. In 2011, Washington was the first state to pass state legislation supporting a trauma-sensitive approach. H.R. 1965 (Wash. 2011) identifies and promotes innovative strategies to prevent and reduce adverse childhood experiences. In 2013 Pennsylvania followed suit, passing H.R. 191 (Penn. 2012), supporting trauma-informed education statewide. In Massachusetts, H.B. 3528 (Mass. 2014) mandating "safe and supportive schools" statewide was signed into law on August 13, 2014.

Assumptions of Trauma-Sensitive Schools

All children are born with fundamental needs for connection, attunement, trust, autonomy, and love. When these needs are met in a predictable and reassuring manner, children learn to test the parameters of dependence and interdependence. The self emerges from this strong foundation, with the confidence it needs to approach learning. Children with a history of positive caregiving are in touch with their body and can regulate their emotions and behavior in a manner that allows them to adjust to changing environmental expectations and achieve their goals. They are able to connect with others as a source of nourishment and comfort.

In the absence of these nurturing relationships, children's ability to achieve these core capacities is compromised. Lacking the protection of responsive caregivers, they develop survival strategies to cope with their feelings of disconnection, dysregulation, disorganization, and isolation. As children mature, these early adaption or survival strategies have a profound impact on children's enthusiasm for life, their resiliency, and their capacity to form meaningful relationships with others (Haller & LaPierre, 2012).

Establishing a link between childhood adversity and subsequent behaviors places the origin of these often hostile behaviors within an interpersonal context. In this model, children's challenging behaviors are seen as a direct or indirect result of an "injury," often inflicted at the hands of a caretaker. These injuries include physical, emotional, and social maltreatment, all of which affect the social interactivity required for healthy brain development. Instead, a series of biological adaptions occur that change the way the brain, the neuroendocrine stress response, and the immune system function, both individually and cooperatively (Johnson, Riley, Granger, & Riis, 2013). These adaptions are essential for children's survival, but they create serious limitations on their ability to cope with the academic and social demands of school.

Components of the Model

The trauma-sensitive framework is flexible, meaning it can be personalized to meet the needs of local school communities (Cole, Eisner, Gregory, & Ristuccia, 2013). There are, however, several model components that facilitate implementation of a trauma-sensitive approach.

Staff Training and Supervision. Teachers and school administrators are trained to view existing supports and interventions through a trauma-sensitive lens. Professional development on the sensory nature of unresolved trauma and how to make accommodations that are responsive to the challenges this presents are routinely provided. Close collaboration with neighborhood mental health agencies ensures the availability of additional resources for children in crisis or whose needs require short-term targeted interventions (Craig, 2008). Trauma-sensitive supervision helps teachers maintain positive relationships with students and avoid falling prey to compassion fatigue or vicarious traumatization (Figley, 2002).

Instruction That Supports Neural Development. Current understanding of the social nature of the brain calls for educators to re-examine instructional frameworks to ensure that they promote children's neural development. Children learn best in environments characterized by safe, caring relationships; meaningful collaboration; and frequent opportunities for multisensory exploration of concepts and ideas. While many recommended practices are compatible with these goals, trauma-sensitive schools rely on differentiated instruction and dialogic teaching because of the clear benefits they offer children with early trauma histories. Differentiated instruction provides children with frequent opportunities to give and receive feedback, thereby allowing teachers to continually adapt instruction to meet a student's changing needs (Tomlinson, 2001). Dialogic teaching offers teachers a framework for addressing the language deficits common among this population of children (Nystrand, 2006). In addition, its commitment to conversational engagement with the teacher supports children's efforts to make connections between language and behavior, correct cognitive distortions, and build personal agency into their explanatory narratives.

Classroom Management. Trauma-sensitive schools use components of positive behavior support (PBS) and social-emotional learning (SEL) to help children achieve self-regulatory behaviors, make positive connections with others, and develop self-esteem. The PBS model is an extension of applied behavior analysis that anticipates when and where problem behaviors may occur throughout the school day (Sugai, Horner, Dunlap, Hieneman, Lewis, Nelson, . . . Ruef, 2000). It is a tiered approach that focuses on preventing behaviors that are inconsistent with school success. School-based teams identify a limited number of developmentally appropriate behaviors that children and staff work on together throughout the day. Expectations are clearly defined and frequently discussed, using a common language that reinforces the model's focus on anticipating and preventing problems. Children can access universal supports—that is, supports needed to meet agreed upon expectations—across all school settings on an as-needed basis. Trauma-sensitive schools emphasize supports that help children manage stress, avoid trauma triggers, and build positive relationships with teachers and peers.

The SEL framework provides teachers with tools they can use to help children recognize their feelings, monitor their behavior, and develop habits of the mind that foster empathy and cooperation (Brackett & Rivers, 2014). Its emphasis on self-awareness is particularly beneficial to children who are impulsive or who are unaware of the effects of their behavior on others. SEL strategies are easily integrated into instruction in any content area. Trauma-sensitive schools rely on these strategies to help children manage the symptoms of anxiety and hyperarousal so often associated with histories of early trauma.

Policies and Procedures. Trauma-sensitive schools are characterized by policies and procedures designed to ensure the safety and success of children with early trauma histories. While physical safety is paramount, the approach also includes strict adherence to confidentiality, as well as protection against bullying and other threats to emotional well-being. Clear rules apply to communication with noncustodial parents, especially when there is a restraining order or a history of domestic violence.

Policies regarding discipline, safety planning, communication, and collaboration with community health organizations benefit not only children with known histories of trauma but also those whose trauma will never be clearly defined, as well as those who may be affected by the behavior of their traumatized classmates (Asam, 2015).

Discipline. Discipline policies in trauma-sensitive schools are proactive, intended to anticipate and prevent as many problems as possible. Staff are trained to implement agreed-upon universal supports in a consistent and timely manner. Teachers articulate and review behavioral expectation with children. The school handles infractions in a collaborative manner that increases children's self-awareness and their ability to monitor their behaviors. Conflicts are resolved in a manner that repairs any harm that occurred.

Collaboration with Community Agencies. To address the mental health needs of children and families with trauma histories or current adversities, trauma-sensitive school policies include protocols that create formal collaborative relationships with community mental health agencies. These partnerships increase opportunities for social-emotional interventions, provide school staff with convenient referral services, and offer training for teachers and school staff.

The benefits of a trauma-sensitive approach go beyond its intended goal of helping traumatized children achieve academic and social competency. The model helps children unaffected by trauma by reducing disruptive behaviors that pose a threat to school safety and often derail classroom instruction and time on task. As teachers learn new strategies to address the needs of traumatized children, they become better equipped to meet the emotional needs of all their students. They are able to garner professional support from their peers and are not afraid to ask for help when they need it.

IMPLICATIONS FOR EDUCATIONAL REFORM

The first step in implementing a trauma-informed approach in schools is to acknowledge the scope of the problem. Although schools have come a long way in normalizing other types of learning and behavior problems, those that appear to be in some way related to family functioning are approached more gingerly, if at all.

This helps explain why school screenings for adverse childhood experiences or developmental histories that include questions about early traumatic experiences are seldom if ever used in schools. In the absence of these data, it is estimated that each year in the United States over one million children are diagnosed with a mental illness or disability that could be better explained by trauma (Leahy, 2015). As a result, many receive special education services or medications that do not meet their needs because they do not treat the underlying trauma.

Rather than turning a blind eye to the adversity in children's lives, staff in trauma-sensitive schools are equipped to give witness to its existence. In this nonstigmatizing environment, children experience a sense of belonging and acceptance that is missing in other environments where they feel marginalized and alone. No longer needing to hide the stress in their lives, they are able to develop the skills they need to move beyond trauma and create a future for themselves. Validating children's life experiences in nonjudgmental ways is the cornerstone of a trauma-sensitive approach.

Creating a Trauma-Sensitive School Climate

The "conspiracy of silence" that surrounds childhood trauma manifests in the way traditional schools respond to its victims. Teachers are hesitant to probe too deeply into the lives of students outside of school, either because they fear reprisal from parents or see it as outside the scope of their work. School counselors and administrators sometimes blame children for their reaction to terrible things that happen to them. This is particularly true when children externalize their reactions to trauma in behaviors that disrupt the school day or derail classroom instruction. Attempts at containing these outbursts frequently result in re-traumatizing consequences, such as time-out, which increase the student's negative arousal (Perry, 2013). Sometimes this road leads to placement in alternative schools or juvenile justice facilities (Levine & Kline, 2006), thus reinforcing children's internal states of helplessness and despair (Long, Fecser, & Brendtro, 1998).

Trauma-sensitive schools provide children with a nurturing, developmentally appropriate, and educationally rich environment that is responsive

WHAT ADMINISTRATORS CAN DO

1. Provide staff with professional development training on how to de-escalate hostile, aggressive behaviors.

2. Provide staff with professional development training on differentiated instruction and dialogic teaching.

3. Provide the leadership needed to help staff arrive at a limited number of developmentally appropriate expectations for children.

4. Review school policies to ensure they reflect a trauma-sensitive discipline and safety.

WHAT TEACHERS CAN DO

1. Willingly collaborate with children to develop the social and regulatory behaviors they need to achieve academic and social mastery.

2. Remain objective when de-escalating with children's aggressive behavior.

3. Use differentiated instruction and dialogic teaching to design lessons that engage children in meaningful activities that foster neural development and higher-order thinking.

4. Use clear, precise language to talk to children about how they can work with you to anticipate and prevent problems.

to their needs (Garbarino, Dubrow, Kostelny, & Pardo, 1992). Within this protective context traumatized children learn to manage the effects of trauma and move on with their lives. The culture of a trauma-sensitive school is strength based. Teachers and administrators emphasize helping children take control of themselves and their learning. Staff are emotionally available to students and are willing collaborators, helping develop the social and regulatory behaviors needed to achieve academic competency. Working together, teachers and administrators commit to bringing a trauma-sensitive perspective to all aspects of school climate: instructional practices, classroom management, policies and procedures, discipline, and collaboration with outside agencies.

CONCLUSION

The prevalence of early childhood trauma among school-aged children threatens their academic and social success. The links between trauma and changes in brain architecture that are detrimental to learning are well established. The trauma-sensitive schools movement represents a national effort to adapt trauma-informed approaches to educational reform. These include designing instruction in a manner that promotes neural development, consistent use of positive behavioral supports, collaboration with community mental health professionals, and creation of a school climate that ensures safety for all children. Staff members are then able to work with the brain's adaptive capacity or neuroplasticity to help children restore their capacity for self-regulation, social connection, and learning. They are able to thrive, not just survive.

CHAPTER 2

Dealing with Student Trauma

A Missing Component of Educational Reform

The only thing harder than starting something new is changing something old.

—Russell Ackoff

The word "traumatic" is often used to describe extraordinary events, such as the September 11, 2001 attack or the Boston Marathon bombing in 2013. This usage is imprecise, however. Events are not traumatic in and of themselves; they become traumatic when they exceed a person's capacity to cope. In other words, trauma depends not only on the event, but also on the absent or limited resources available to help a person respond to the situation, manage, and return to a sense of calmness and control.

This chapter describes the effects of early trauma on children's development. Research documenting its high prevalence in childhood adversity is presented, as well as an overview of the symptoms of complex, developmental trauma. Emphasis is placed on the role the environment plays in shaping the brain's architecture, and the restorative effects of neuroplasticity.

THE HIGH COST OF TRAUMA ON CHILDREN'S LIVES

Because children depend so much on their caregivers, they are especially vulnerable to complex trauma if their early relationships with these caregivers are marred by neglect or other types of maltreatment. Developmentally adverse experiences evoke the same level of anxiety in children as that experienced by adults in situations that are imminently life threatening. Some early childhood trauma occurs as the result of accidents, medical procedures, or community violence. The vast majority of childhood trauma, however, takes place at home. Almost always the people responsible for child maltreatment are parents and primary caregivers (van der Kolk, 2005). As a result, these traumas are often unseen or unrecognized by anyone outside the child's home.

Evidence from Divergent Sources of Trauma's Debilitating Effects

Evidence from three separate, but closely related, lines of work on adverse childhood experiences (Felitti et al., 1998), poly-victimization (Finkelhor, Ormod, & Turner, 2007), and cumulative trauma (Briere & Spinazzola, 2005; Cloitre, Stolbach, Herman, van der Kolk, Pynoos, Wang, & Petkova, 2009) provide strong support for a correlation between early childhood trauma and subsequent learning problems, as well as increased risk of mental and physical illness. The ability of neuroscience to map the neurological changes that occur as the result of trauma moves the findings of these studies beyond association to causation disorders (Perry, 2002). In other words, there are now hard data for previously hypothesized correlations. Once understood, this link between cause and effect can help educators change school climate, instructional design, and behavior management and thereby build the capacity of all children to reach their full potential.

With a sample size of over 17,000 well-educated, middle-class adults, the Adverse Childhood Experiences (ACE) study provides substantial evidence of the role that trauma and cumulative stress plays on increasing the risk of disease, disability, and early mortality (Felitti et al., 1998). Conducted by Kaiser Permanente and the Centers for Disease Control and Prevention, the ACE study is distinguished from earlier investigations of the relationship between trauma and disease or dysfunction in three important ways. First, it looks only at interpersonal adversity, excluding other traumatic events such as accidents, natural disaster, and illness. Second, it increases the range of potentially traumatic experiences to include household dysfunction and family mental health, as well as examples of abuse and neglect. Third, it looks at the cumulative effects of repeated "hidden stressors" rather than single traumatic events.

The ACE study shows that adverse childhood experiences are much more common than recognized or previously acknowledged. The results offer substantial evidence that chronic stress at an early age overtaxes the body's biological systems and alters a host of stress-related responses in ways that are detrimental to development. The original ACEs pyramid showed scientific gaps where scientists noted the correlations were unable to explain the outcomes (see Figure 2.1).

The recently revised pyramid (see Figure 2.2) reflects scientific breakthroughs in the understanding of how chronic childhood adversity affects early childhood brain development (Center for Youth Wellness, 2014). A

Figure 2.1. Original ACEs Pyramid

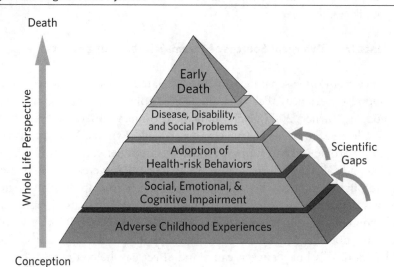

Figure 2.2. Revised ACE Pyramid

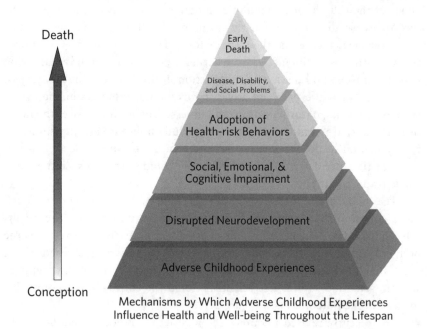

Mechanisms by Which Adverse Childhood Experiences
Influence Health and Well-being Throughout the Lifespan

Figure 2.3. Types of Adverse Childhood Experiences

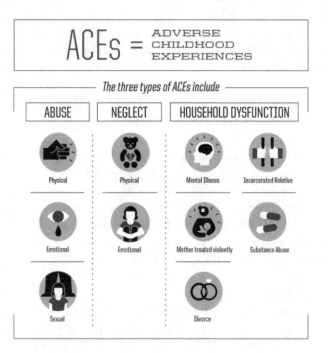

child's brain will make early accommodations to ensure survival and adaptation to stressful situations, and these accommodations undermine the progressive construction of the brain's complex neural networks responsible for memory, learning, motivation, information processing, problem solving, and distress tolerance (Belsky & Haan, 2011). These effects are not only emotional or psychological; they are also biological, and they put traumatized children at a significant disadvantage, particularly with regard to their ability to succeed at school.

The ACE study looks at 10 childhood situations, categorized into three types: abuse, neglect, and household dysfunction (see Figure 2.3).

The Multiple Effects of Poly-victimization

The term *poly-victimization* grew out of a large, nationally representative random-digit dialing survey of caregivers of children ages 2–9 and adolescents 10–17 (Finkelhor, Turner, Ormod, & Hamby, 2010). Victimization was measured using the Juvenile Victimization Questionnaire (JVQ)

(Hamby, Finkelhor, Turner, & Kracke, 2011). As in the ACE study, the authors focused on only interpersonal events and the effects of multiple or cumulative incidences of victimization. The results were similar. The JVQ study demonstrated that, when estimating children's risk for the symptoms of posttraumatic stress disorder (PTSD), researchers need to consider the total number of ways children were victimized within a calendar rather than focusing on any single type alone (Finkelhor et al., 2010).

The Cumulative Effects of Repeated Trauma

The effects of trauma on children's learning and behavior are cumulative. Multiple exposures to interpersonal trauma, such as abandonment, betrayal, physical or sexual assaults, or exposure to domestic violence have consistent and predictable consequences. These affect many areas of functioning that have serious ramifications for future academic and social mastery. A deep-seated distrust of adults, coupled with a hypersensitivity to perceptions of danger or threat, seriously compromise children's ability to learn. Instead of integrating new information or experience, their attention is directed at survival and defending themselves against reoccurring trauma symptoms such as heightened arousal or dissociation. Some children avoid situations that precipitate these symptoms. Others try to project some sense of control over potential danger or threats. These children *reenact* their traumas through aggressive or sexual acting-out behaviors. Others develop *somatic problems*, such as headaches and stomachaches, in response to fearful and helpless emotions.

The greater the number of different types of trauma children are exposed to, the greater the number of developmental domains affected, causing these children to manifest multiple symptoms. Although trauma's impact is most pervasive during the first decade of a child's life, these experiences set the stage for lifelong unfocused responses to stress because chronic trauma interferes with neurobiological development (van der Kolk, 2005) and the development of core self-regulation capacities (Ford & Russo, 2006). Children's capacity to integrate sensory, emotional, and cognitive information in new situations is compromised by their brain's response to traumatic events in the past.

Early efforts to arrive at a precise diagnosis of cumulative trauma in children were hampered by the vast array of developmental consequences. Multiple discrete diagnoses of problems such as attention deficit disorder, speech delay, and oppositional-defiant behavior obscure the pattern of trauma-related disturbances that are part of a pervasive disorder that needs to be addressed in an integrated manner (van der Kolk, 2005).

In 2005, members of the National Child Traumatic Stress Network (NCTSN, 2005) came together to develop a more precise diagnosis for children with early trauma histories. Referred to as developmental trauma disorder (DTD), the provisional diagnosis is organized around the issues of "triggered dysregulation in response to traumatic reminders, stimulus generalization, and the anticipatory organization of behavior to prevent the recurrence of the trauma impact" (van der Kolk, 2005, p. 582). These manifest in school as poor self-regulation and a propensity toward apparently unprovoked aggressive behavior, a pervasive mistrust of authority figures, and a hypersensitivity to danger that limits children's motivation and ability to learn.

Shaping the Brain's Architecture

The converging evidence of the ACE and JVQ studies, combined with research on the consequences of cumulative trauma, makes the negative impact of early adversity on children's lives impossible to ignore. Given the prevalence of early childhood trauma among school-aged children, educators need strategies to help children overcome the negative effects of their early life experiences. Overall this means helping teachers appreciate the brain's never-ending plasticity—its capacity to change within the context of nurturing, social relationships.

The Environment's Role in Neural Development

The environment exerts a tremendous influence on the brain's structure and chemistry, to the point of affecting gene expression or suppression (Peckham, 2013). It is important for teachers to understand how persistent adversity weakens the brain's operating system as well as how healthy, stimulating school experiences can help children create compensatory strategies that allow them to reach their highest potential.

In terms of children's academic and social mastery, trauma's effects on the brain's horizontal and vertical organization, as well as the restorative effects of engagement and neuroplasticity, are of particular interest.

Horizontal Organization. The brain's horizontal organization consists of a left and a right hemisphere. Information is exchanged across the hemispheres via a thick band of fiber called the corpus callosum. Maltreatment in early childhood results in reduced left hemisphere volume, as well as changes in the composition of the middle section of the corpus callosum, suggesting inadequate integration of the left and right hemispheres. As a result, children's emotions are compartmentalized. While positive feelings are processed in the left hemisphere, negative or hostile feelings are experienced in the right hemisphere (Teicher, 2000). In other words, traumatized children are unable to use language and reasoning to manage the heightened reactivity of their right hemisphere (Cook, Blaustein, Spinazzola, & van der Kolk, 2003). As a result, their feelings of uncontrollable helplessness and rage are bound to be repeated.

Vertical Organization. The brain's vertical organization is from bottom to top, beginning with the inner lower brain stem and moving up through the limbic or midbrain section to the outer higher cortical areas and prefrontal cortex. The brain stem, often referred to as the reptilian brain, regulates body function and energy flow. It directly affects arousal and is the arbitrator of the body's stress response. The amygdala and hippocampus are located in the limbic area, which is located directly above the brain stem. The amygdala is the body's "first responder" to danger, immediately triggering a sense of fear, which in turn results in a heightened level of arousal. Although the hippocampus has the capacity to evaluate perceived dangers, comparing them to other similar experiences, it is slow to develop and therefore incapable of preventing prolonged alarm reactions in young children.

The protective environment of closely attuned relationships between children and their caregivers provides initial regulation of the child's stress response. Rapid, predictable responses to children's needs lead to the formation of moderate to high levels of stress tolerance in the brain stem and limbic area. Working together, children and caregivers establish a pattern of comfortable state regulation that reduces the incidence of impulsive or reactive behaviors.

Infants whose early relationships with caregivers are characterized by high levels of adversity or trauma adapt to these circumstances with a heightened level of arousal, a low threshold for stress tolerance, and greater reactivity in the brain stem and limbic areas. These adaptive changes produce an attentional bias toward threat or danger that over time results in a permanent state of hyperarousal and dysregulation. Unlike peers whose experiences of heightened arousal are short-lived with a return to normal once a threat is removed, the early experiences of traumatized children permanently change the reactivity of their lower brain. What begins as a protective adaptation becomes an impediment to self-regulation and learning.

As a result, it is more difficult for the cortex or higher brain to oversee and control brain stem activity. These early changes to the brain's architecture make it harder for children to pause before acting, have insight

---

WHAT ADMINISTRATORS CAN DO

1. Provide the needed leadership to help staff understand children's behavior as coping strategies designed to survive earlier adversity and trauma.

2. Provide teachers with professional development focused on recognizing and responding to symptoms of childhood trauma.

3. Eliminate discipline practices that may trigger symptoms in children with early trauma histories: public reprimands, time-out, zero-tolerance policies.

4. Get to know the children in your school. Greet them at the beginning and end of each day, and address them by name when passing them in hallways. Repeated positive acknowledgment can help lessen their distrust and fear of authority figures.

5. Collaborate with local community organizations to create wraparound services for families and children who need them.

6. Provide teachers with professional development on how trauma affects the horizontal and vertical organization of children's brains.

7. Sponsor schoolwide change contests. Have classroom teams works together to identify something they would like to change in their environment and design a plan to make it happen.

8. Schedule time for teachers to participate in professional learning communities or other interactive forums that encourage them to integrate trauma-sensitive approaches into their classroom practice.

---

and empathy, and enact moral judgments (Siegel, 2010). Their capacity to coordinate their thinking, emotional regulation, and behavior is seriously diminished.

Poverty as Environmental Trauma

Effective educational reform requires a better understanding of the relationship between poverty, trauma, and disruptions in neurobiological development. The harrowing effects of chronic poverty are not limited to economic disparity. Rather, they are exacerbated by the pervasive trauma and disorganization poverty produces within a child's family structure and home environment.

Prolonged financial insecurity triggers a host of life-conditioning experiences that erode the protective capacity of the family in ways that traumatize

---

WHAT TEACHERS CAN DO

1. Become knowledgeable about the ways childhood trauma affects children's ability to achieve academic and social mastery.

2. Support children's efforts to acquire the self-awareness and self-monitoring skills needed for self-regulation.

3. Integrate self-soothing activities like movement, music, and deep breathing into classroom activities and routines.

4. Collaborate with children to help them manage their emotional reactions and maintain an optimal level of arousal.

5. Monitor the length and complexity of homework assignments to reduce unnecessary stress for children whose caregivers are unavailable to help them.

6. Provide children with time to regain their composure before asking them to use language to explain misbehavior.

7. Design instruction that works with the brain's plasticity to strengthen the neural pathways associated with higher-order thinking.

8. Use classroom activities to foster positive relationships and social support among peers.

---

both parents and their children. Poor people are overly stressed and often lack the resources they need to adequately meet daily demands (Babcock, 2014). Inadequate housing, unpredictable food supply, transportation issues, crime, and lack of physical safety undermine parental effectiveness and limit siblings' ability to care for one another. The result is a pattern of trauma-organized behavior that impairs family functioning and alters children's neurological development.

Children rely on the adults around them to interpret disturbing or threatening experiences in a reassuring manner that quickly re-establishes safety. For many parents, the inherent stress of living in chronic poverty negatively affects their ability to make decisions or solve problems (Babcock, 2014). Their higher-order thinking or executive functioning skills are hijacked by the struggle to survive. They find it difficult to appropriately modulate their behavior or set goals (Casey, Jones, & Somerville, 2011). The massive cognitive load imposed on them by poverty leaves little "bandwidth" to do many of the things needed to improve their situation (Badger, 2013). They are unable to imagine a way out. Futility is the hallmark of their daily lives.

It is this intersection of poverty and trauma that is so detrimental to children. The dependent status of children means that they are subject to the circumstances of their parents' lives (van der Kolk, 2005). A recent article in *JAMA Pediatrics* documents the same anomalies in neural development among children living in chronic poverty and children exposed to other forms of toxic stress such as maltreatment or community violence (Luby, Belden, Botteron, Marrus, Harms, Babb, . . . Barch, 2013). Similarly, the 2012 Urban ACE Study in Philadelphia found that the ACE scores of adults living in poverty were significantly higher than those of the middle-class participants in the original 1998 Kaiser Permanente Study (Taylor, 2013).

When the hassle of daily life limits caregivers' ability to shield children from adversity and stress, the children are left with little or no "buffer zone" to safeguard their development. They adapt in a manner that favors their survival but threatens their ability to succeed in school.

Restorative Effects of Engagement and Neuroplasticity

While optimal brain maturation occurs within the context of caring, predictable relationships, interventions that make use of the brain's neuroplasticity can dramatically reduce the effects of early trauma. The brain's ability to benefit from enriching environmental experiences offers new hope for the thousands of children whose early life experiences are marred by adversity and trauma. Schools can become healing environments for troubled children when teachers understand the role the environment plays in neural development and the anomalies caused by early trauma histories. This knowledge allows them to design instruction that works with the brain's plasticity to establish and strengthen the neural pathways associated with academic and social competency.

The brain's neurobiology holds the secret to successful educational reform. But it must first be understood by teachers and embraced by those with the authority to effect change. "Because early experiences occur within the context of a developing brain, neural development and social interaction are inextricably mixed" (Tucker, 1992, p. 576). It is the social nature of children's brains, and the relational trajectory by which they grow, that determines their academic and social competency.

Schools that are attuned to these new developments in brain science make great strides in resolving the problems that continue to plague education today: closing the achievement gap between the rich and poor, improving the behavior and social competency of children who appear recalcitrant and defiant, reducing the dropout rate, and improving the quality of children's lives overall.

IMPLICATIONS FOR EDUCATIONAL REFORM

Trauma-sensitive intervention requires the formation of collaborative relationships between traumatized children and adults who can help them develop the emotional regulation needed to control precipitous behavioral changes caused by environmental triggers. With the correct type of support, children can learn ways of using self-monitoring and cognitive control to make informed choices about their behavior. Stress management and self-soothing activities can help them build their tolerance for discomfort and maintain a more functional level of arousal.

CONCLUSION

The high prevalence of trauma among school-aged children, as well as its effects on development, is well documented. Experiences of early adversity produce high levels of anxiety in children, which trigger neurological changes in their stress response. These changes undermine the maturation of the neural networks that contribute to academic and social mastery. Children's capacity to integrate new knowledge and experiences is compromised by their brains' response to traumatic events in the past. To be effective, efforts at educational reform must address these pervasive trauma-related disorders. Implementation of this trauma-sensitive approach will restore children's capacity to regulate their emotions and participate successfully in school.

CHAPTER 3

The Neurology of Attachment

Caregiving Counts

The test of the morality of a society is what it does for its children.

—*Dietrich Bonhoeffer*

During infancy the brain is typically only a quarter of its adult size. A large part of its development takes place within the context of children's early relationships (Lieberman & Van Horn, 2013). Within these relationships, the primary caregiver's attunement to the infant's needs and desires supports the development of the central nervous system (CNS) and autonomic nervous system (ANS).

The brain's architecture is socially constructed within the context of a child's first attachment relationship. For healthy development, an infant's brain literally requires programming by a loving adult's eyes and facial expressions. Unless the child has easy access to responsive caregivers, the neural pathways and processes needed to mediate physical and mental health will not mature. The effects of these early care-receiving experiences influence every aspect of children's development, including genetic expression (Crespi, 2011), and neural plasticity, or the brain's ability to change and adapt to environmental or behavioral shifts (Rapoport & Gogtay, 2008).

This chapter presents an overview of how development occurs through a dynamic relationship between the brain, mind, and body of both the infant and caregiver, held within an environment that supports and protects the bonding process. Strategies teachers can use to foster secure relationships with students are provided, as well as an explanation of how early relationships affect the development of the neural pathways needed for self-regulation and pragmatic language.

THE EFFECTS OF TRAUMA ON CHILDREN'S
ATTACHMENT RELATIONSHIPS

The essential task of the first year of life is the creation of a secure attachment bond between the infant and the primary caregiver. This process involves frequent physical contact and affectionate communication between caregivers and infants. Each learns the rhythmic structure of the other, and modifies his or her behavior to fit that structure. The result is a specifically fitted attachment interaction between the individual child and the individual primary caregiver.

Learning to Attach

Bruce Perry defines the attachment process as the "emotional glue" needed for future relationships (Perry, 2013, p. 2). The capacity and desire to relate to others depends on the organization and functioning of specific parts of the brain that develop in this process. It requires caregiver attunement to the infant's changing needs, coupled with the ability to match the child's affect, attention, and gestures. Mirroring infants' vocalizations and movements reinforces the sense of connection between the caregiver and the child. When both infant and caregiver focus on the same object or event, the sense of reciprocity and shared intention between them is strengthened. These episodes of joint attention start with the caregiver following the infant's eye gaze. The two then engage in a conversation about what the baby is looking at. The willingness of the caregiver to pick up on the infant's interest, labeling and describing it, contributes to the child's language development and sense of personal agency.

Attachment patterns develop as caregivers help children construct the explanatory narrative that defines their experience and forms their sense of identity or self-definition. The way children remember the events of their lives impacts their ability to cope with present and future stressors. The structure and content of parent-guided reminiscing reflects the caregiver's own coping skills and attachment status. Secure attachment results when children sense the caregiver as available and competent, the self as worthy of care, and the world as safe and secure. It requires a high degree of caregiver attunement to the nonverbal expressions of the infant's arousal and affective state. Caregivers are able to appraise and respond to the child's needs, regulate them, and communicate them back to the infant as manageable and under control.

Secure attachment relationships are characterized by an interactive synchronicity that helps parent and child maintain a level of positive arousal that encourages curiosity and learning. Reliance on the caregiver as a secure base enables children to physically explore their environment, knowing they can return to the safety of their caregiver's presence. With enough repetition, a sense of security is firmly established. Even when miscues or misunderstandings occur, the caregiver can regulate the infant's negative state by repairing the misunderstanding in a timely manner.

Trauma and neglect mar the attachment relationship in ways that make it difficult for caregivers to provide children with this type of co-regulation. The inability of caregivers to provide timely and consistent feedback to children results in a pattern of insecure attachment. As a result, children lack a sense of internal control, also referred to as personal agency. Powerless in the face of their caregivers' unpredictability, they create explanatory narratives characterized by feelings of helplessness and despair. They are unable to set future goals or try new roles. They show little interest in learning new things.

Attachment Patterns and Neuroplasticity

Brain plasticity refers to the brain's necessary capacity to change as a result of input from the environment. Brain circuits are built in a bottom-up sequence over the course of the developmental period between infancy and age 5. The brain is most plastic during the early period of development, meaning that during this time it is the most vulnerable to the effects of attachment failures that threaten neural development. As brain circuits stabilize, they become increasingly difficult to alter. The window of opportunity for neuroplasticity is 0–5 years, because of the synaptic (strength of connection between brain cells) and cellular (number of brain cell connections or synapses) changes that occur during that period. Neuronal connections (see Figure 3.1) develop in a use-dependent manner. The more often they are used, the stronger they become. In infancy, the brain is making 1,000 connections per second, more than at any other period of life.

This rapid growth in early childhood has both a positive and a negative side. The positive side is that young children's brains are primed to benefit from enriching, developmentally appropriate learning environments. The negative side is this openness to learning makes young children's brains more vulnerable to developmental problems in impoverished or threatening environments. But even then, because cellular development is use dependent, children are capable of recovery given intense early intervention that repairs the attachment relationship so that more positive neuronal connections can be made.

Children who experience attachment failures in their early relationships can learn to draw comfort and support from teachers and others they

Figure 3.1. Neuronal Connections

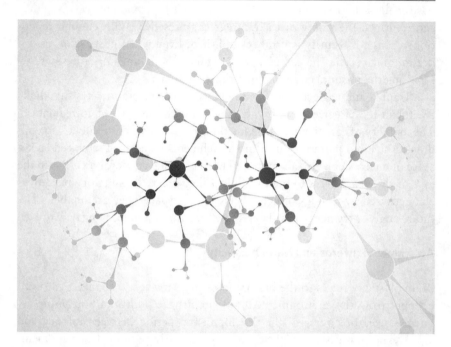

encounter later in childhood, provided their patterns of insecurity are recognized and responded to in a manner that repairs early damage. Children manifest the results of early childhood trauma in two extreme ways: either they resist adult engagement in ways that seem sullen and remote, or they attach too readily, clinging to anyone who displays even the slightest attention to them. Teachers need to be especially mindful of children who demonstrate an apparent lack of interest in them. It is all too common for adults to respond to disinterested children with similar in-kind behaviors. This further inhibits any interest they may have in others. What they need instead is sustained contact with adults who show an unwavering interest in them. This can increase their ability to respond to another's efforts to engage them, which in turn helps sustain their curiosity and their ability to learn.

Although many children with attachment issues avoid contact with others, some display what is referred to as *indiscriminant proximity seeking* (Schuengel, Oosterman, & Sterkenburg, 2009). These are children who bond too easily with anyone who shows the slightest interest in them. This puts them at risk for maltreatment by peers, as well as adult predators who recognize their vulnerability. These children benefit from collaborative

Figure 3.2. Limbic Area of Right Hemisphere

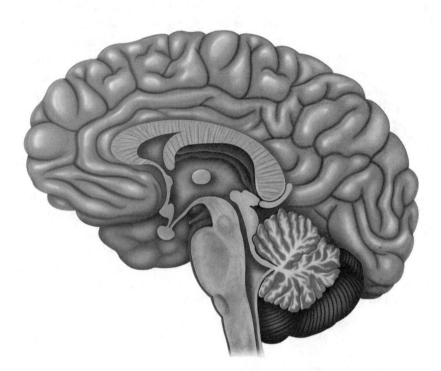

relationships with adults who are able to set and maintain appropriate boundaries.

Right Hemisphere Development

Attachment relationships shape the unconscious self-system of the brain's right hemisphere (see Figure 3.2). This evolves in the preverbal stages of development. The impact these relationships have on the cortical and limbic autonomic right cerebral hemisphere involves far more than the fundamental sense of safety and security usually associated with it.

These relationships shape the preverbal matrix of one's core sense of self that evolves into the dynamic unconsciousness (Schore & Schore, 2008). This nonverbal self-definition unconsciously guides the individual in interpersonal contexts throughout life. The encoded strategies of affective regulation learned in infancy become the building blocks of children's self-regulation.

Because of the essentially collaborative nature of the attachment process, when caregivers themselves have trauma histories, their own disorganized, insecure attachment patterns are affectively burned into the infant's developing right brain (Schore, 2001, 2003). Caregivers' inappropriate or rejecting responses to infants' needs induce traumatic states of enduring negative affect in the infant. These interfere with the development of the arousal-regulating process. Instead of playing a modulating role in helping infants manage their internal needs, caregivers induce an extremely high level of stimulation and arousal, as in the case of abuse, or extremely low levels in the case of neglect.

Trauma has the unfortunate effect of leaving children in the past, unable to move forward. Instead, experiences in the present trigger the sensations and feelings of past traumas over which they had no control. The result is that traumatized children are thrown back into their past and compulsively reenact earlier events.

When traumatized children experience vehement emotions, their minds are often incapable of matching their frightening experiences with reassuring cognitive schemas. Their recollections of past traumatic experiences and emotions remain embedded within the right hemisphere, influencing behavior, although lacking the language necessary to explain or articulate them. The memories remain split off from consciousness and voluntary control. When triggered, they result in extreme, inexplicable, and overwhelming emotional arousal. This reaction is caused by partial or complete loss of the normal integration between memories of the past, awareness of the self in real time, and immediate sensations and control of bodily movement.

ATTACHMENTS AT SCHOOL

Children with histories of insecure attachment display a variety of behaviors toward teachers that parallel their behavior toward their primary caregivers. Some avoid direct contact with teachers, seeking connection instead through showing an interest in classroom materials. Others resist compliance with classroom activities and routines, are easily frustrated, and appear to seek teacher attention through fussy or irritable behaviors. Forming relationships with these children requires keen powers of observation and the ability to tune into their feelings and fear in a manner that conveys safety and reassurance rather than reinforcing negative patterns.

Attunement: A Two-Pronged Process

The same attunement process that enables secure attachment in infants is the basis for positive teacher–child relationships in school. Teachers use the attributes of playfulness, acceptance, curiosity, and empathy to observe children's nonverbal communication, and eventually engage them in reciprocal interactions. They use nonverbal cues of their own such as eye contact, affect matching, and gesture matching to convey respect for children, as well as their willingness to collaborate with them.

Attachment relationships with teachers benefit all children, but especially those with histories of maltreatment or other types of early trauma. These children often expect adults to dislike or reject them. Over time, positive interactions with teachers change children's expectations of relationships and give them the security they need to explore new concepts and behaviors. Teachers can use these relationships to model appropriate social behaviors and improve children's ability to regulate their feelings and behavior.

Teachers in trauma-sensitive schools are aware of the effects of trauma on relationships and learning. They use this knowledge to engage students in activities that give them a sense of mastery and pleasure, while avoiding pursuits that trigger trauma reactions. They understand their role as an attachment figure, and realize that children's early attachment experiences affect their capacity to create and sustain positive relationships.

Trauma-sensitive teachers remain objective about children's behavior and redirect them in a manner that prevents reenactments of earlier negative experiences with adults. They are able to receive and express nonverbal affective communication and engage children in an empathic manner. They provide students with direct instruction in how the stress response works and provide them with alternative strategies to avoid their habitual fight, flight, or freeze reactions. Over time, students learn how to enjoy pleasurable activities without becoming overwhelmed and dysregulated.

Reducing New Traumatic Exposure

The quality of children's early caregiving experiences produce one of two relational systems—high-quality relationships produce a social system for bonding and getting close, whereas less adequate care results in a hierarchical system characterized by rules for keeping your distance and knowing your place (Hughes & Baylin, 2012). Quality caregiving experiences result in bonded relationships that facilitate the development of five interacting neural systems that increase children's understanding of themselves and others. These include (1) the social approach system that allows children to approach others without becoming defensive, (2) the social reward system that makes interactions enjoyable, (3) the people-reading systems that help children interpret nonverbal communication and predict what others may do next, (4) the meaning-making system that helps children make sense of their social world, and (5) the executive system that regulates interpersonal conflict and maintains a balance between prosocial and defensive behaviors (Hughes & Baylin, 2012).

Less-than-adequate care shifts the dynamic between parent and child from a bonding relational system to the creation of a social hierarchy relational system characterized by power-based ranking relationships. Children raised in social hierarchy relational systems are less in tune with themselves and others, and have fewer ways of resolving conflicts.

Unfortunately, public schools often opt for behavior management techniques and discipline policies that reinforce the social hierarchy relational system. The school structures and teachers do not present opportunities to attach (Bergin & Bergin, 2009). When events at school reinforce past negative experiences, they do nothing to reduce the effects of trauma in children's lives. Children with early trauma histories continue to perceive adults as untrustworthy and the world as unfair. They are unable to overcome past attachment failures that limit their academic and social mastery.

Staff in trauma-sensitive schools know that many children's early care results in expectations of a hierarchical relational system. They avoid classroom-management techniques that are authoritarian or harsh in nature. Instead, teachers use a combination of brain-based strategies like playfulness, acceptance, curiosity, and empathy to "surprise" children's mistrusting brains by challenging their expectations of adult behavior (Hughes & Baylin, 2012). This is the first step in building collaborative relationships that prevent the triggering of old traumas. As bonds between teachers and children develop, the children eventually generalize a feeling of attachment to their school. Children who feel bonded to their school feel a sense of belonging, knowing that "the people in my school like me" (Bergin & Bergin, 2009).

Enhancing Protective Factors

School experiences help children compensate for early attachment failures by providing them with a protective environment designed to reshape their perceptions of themselves and others. In addition to buffering the effects of insecure attachment on children's achievement, quality relationships with teachers can inspire children to have a higher opinion of themselves (O'Connor & McCartney, 2007). This occurs when high expectations for performance and behavior are paired with the scaffolds and accommodations children need to achieve them.

Student–teacher collaboration provides an excellent framework for modeling problem-solving strategies, including the need for persistence and optimism when faced with obstacles in meeting a desired goal. This type of collaborative relationship helps children learn to generate alternative solutions to challenging situations. With enough practice, they are able to achieve the cognitive flexibility needed to negotiate the demands of everyday life.

Opportunities such as peer tutoring, or working on community outreach projects like food and clothing drives, teach children how to care for and participate with others. These experiences are particularly valuable when adults take the time to acknowledge the child's involvement and let them know how their contributions benefit others. Adult survivors of childhood trauma are quick to note that assuming a caregiving role toward others helped them overcome early adversity.

Barriers to Successful Attachment

Disruptions in the attachment relationships occur when problems exist that threaten the caregivers' attachment capabilities. These can be the result of economic hardship that limits the time and energy caregivers have available to share with their children. Mental health issues present another barrier to successful attachment due to the limits they place on caregivers' consistency and emotional availability. Epigenetics, or the changes in genetic expression due to environmental factors, also plays a role when the caregivers' own early attachment relationships limit their ability to provide quality experiences for their children.

Economic. Children living in chronic poverty are more at risk for insecure attachment than children from middle-class homes. They experience less parental support and are parented in a less collaborative manner than more affluent children, whose caregivers tend to have fewer demands on time and energy that limit their responsiveness to their children. When caregivers are forced to focus on making ends meet, they frequently miss opportunities to help a child establish the neural networks necessary for self-regulation and language development.

These early attachment failures mark the beginning of a trajectory of underachievement and social problems that limit children's ability to do well in school. It is difficult for them to develop positive relationships, and they perceive themselves as being less accepted and having fewer friends than their peers (Rosenfeld, Richman, & Bowen, 2000). Many poor children lack the confidence of those who are securely attached to their caregivers. The chronic stress of their everyday lives is evident in behaviors that reflect a sense of helplessness and despair. They are often criticized for their lack of persistence and grit, when in reality they are often managing home responsibilities that far exceed what is appropriate for their age and level of development.

Emotional. Healthy attachment relationships rely on the emotional availability of the primary caregiver. Caregivers who have histories of secure attachment experiences are able to offer infants the predictability and emotional attunement necessary to establish a similar sense of safety and well-being. Caregivers with flawed attachment experiences of their own have a harder time responding to the infant's needs in a consistent and timely fashion. While still capable of forming organized attachment relationships, their lack of attunement and unreliable behavior often leads to avoidant or ambivalent attachment behaviors in their children.

Children with avoidant attachment appear emotionally distant. They show little affect, although research shows that their internal state is in a constant state of hyperarousal (van der Kolk, 2014). Their early experiences often lack pleasurable "serve and return" exchanges where caregivers use their facial expressions and voice to establish a soothing sense of reciprocity between the two. Avoidant attachment causes children to feel unnoticed. While internally craving attention, they do nothing to demand it. They have difficulty seeking help from others or relying on social support.

Ambivalent attachment is more dramatic. Children engaged in this type of attachment relationship are quite good at drawing attention to themselves by crying, screaming, or having tantrums. Although they seem to derive little comfort from the caregiver's proximity, they maintain an unwavering focus on him or her.

Ambivalent attachment heightens children's anxiety and can inhibit their ability to take risks or explore their environment. Their hypervigilant attention to the caregiver limits their ability to pursue their own interests with peers.

Although children demonstrating avoidant or ambivalent attachment lack the security of their more reciprocally attached peers, most can adapt to the expectations of the school environment. For children whose caregivers continue to suffer the effects of chronic toxic stress, however, the consequences of flawed attachment inhibit success at school. Issues of domestic violence, mental illness, or an unresolved traumatic past so preoccupy the caregivers' attention that they are emotionally unavailable to join with or engage their children in infancy. Within this context, the infant faces the untenable situation of needing the caregiver for survival but being unable to attract his or her attention. The infant's inability to get a response has a shattering effect on the attachment process, resulting in a disorganized pattern of attachment that leaves the infant terrified of the caregiver and others who assume a similar role. Lacking any sense of internal security, these children trust no one. Their explanatory narrative is marred by perceptions of themselves as deficient and ineffective. These feelings, coupled with an inability to regulate their emotions, set the stage for academic and social failure. These children are prone to acting-out behaviors and are skilled at engaging unsuspecting adults into "reenactments" of their original attachment failure by pushing them to a point of rejecting or harmful behaviors that mimic those of their primary caregiver.

Epigenetic. Children's early attachment relationships are the context in which the connective fibers of the brain grow and develop. These brain connections are dependent on "brain to brain" interactions with caregivers whose own neural connections are well established (Hughes & Baylin, 2012). Unfortunately, when parents experienced poor care as children they are unable to provide required nurturing to their own offspring. This problem is not due to poor modeling or lack of motivation; rather, it is biological. The poor quality of care received by the caregiver in childhood "silenced" the expression of oxytocin and genes involved in the formation of strong neural connections between parent and child (Hughes & Baylin, 2012). In other words, nature and nurture are intricately linked by the effect parental behavior has on children's genetic expression. These behaviors do not alter the genetic code, but they do change children's genetic inheritance by suppressing the expression of certain genes. For example, repetitive, highly stressful experiences can cause epigenetic changes that damage neural circuits that help manage and respond to life's adversity (National Scientific Council on the Developing Child, 2010). These "epigenetic" changes are then transmitted across generations.

The epigenetic effects of early abuse or neglect on gene expression helps explain why harsh, abusive, or neglectful parenting appears to run in families (Sigelman & Rider, 2015). Once introduced, violence shifts the dynamics between parents and children from bonding to establishing a power-based social hierarchy. The expression of bond-forming oxytocin is suppressed, while the activity of stress hormones is enhanced (Hughes & Baylin, 2012). Children trying to manage this type of hostile environment have no clear strategy for responding to caregivers or for managing the adversity in their lives. Their efforts at attachment are conflicted and usually unsuccessful. Instead, they are invested in keeping their distance and engaging in self-defending behaviors. They are difficult to engage and, without intervention, at high risk for self-destructive behavior.

ATTACHMENT AND BEHAVIOR

Children's early attachment relationships predict the trajectory of their future ability to get along with others and have positive social interactions. Children with secure attachment histories have the confidence and problem-solving skills needed to meet the academic and social demands of school. Those with insecure attachment patterns are inclined to behave in ways that are less confident and sometimes self-defeating. Self-regulation is often a problem for these children. Some behave aggressively, whereas others are anxious and easily frustrated. In either case, they need reparative experiences that help them move beyond their early attachment failures.

Arousal/Self-Regulation

Self-regulation requires children to have the ability to monitor their behavior and adjust it to meet the expectations of the environment around them. It involves reflection as well as the ability to use self-comforting strategies to keep internal arousal at a manageable level. Some children find physical movements like swinging or rocking comforting. Others find listening to music or physical proximity to a trusted friend calms them down and helps them relax. Acquiring this skill necessitates collaboration with caring adults who are more concerned about understanding children's internal state than they are about complying with disciplinary rules.

Collaborative models of discipline mark a notable shift away from more traditional paradigms such as Lemov's Taxonomy (Lemov, 2010), the broken window theory (Wilson & Kelling, 1982), or the federal government's policy of zero tolerance (Noguera, 1995). These existing models require immediate, often coercive, consequences for noncompliant behaviors without any investigation into the child's motivation. Each time these policies are enforced, teachers and school administrators miss an opportunity to partner with children and to help them tap into their cerebral cortex or higher brain to regulate their level of arousal. In fact, these disciplinary policies reinforce the reactive survival mechanism of the lower brain and prevent the child from moving forward.

Motivation

In positive attachment relationships, adults collaborate in ways that encourage children to have positive attitudes toward themselves and others. Without this support, children are more likely to be pessimistic and unhappy. Children with early trauma histories often develop an attentional bias toward the negative things in their life, meaning that they see their stresses and problems more often and more clearly than they see their successes and opportunities for joy. They are more likely to display anxiety or avoidance behaviors such as getting out of their seat to sharpen a pencil or get a drink of water rather than beginning an assignment. They need more reassurance than peers and more opportunities to practice the art of positive thinking.

Helping children acquire a more optimistic outlook requires collaborating with them to expand their explanatory narrative to include a sense of personal agency, as well as the ability to imagine a future. Overcoming this pervasive sense of pessimism is never easy. It involves engaging children in a manner that helps strengthen their prefrontal cortex through repeated opportunities to set goals, to make choices about goal-related behaviors, and to evaluate the efficacy of their choices. This sequence can be integrated into instructional activities throughout the day and reflects best educational practices known to increase critical thinking skills.

Language plays an important role in building a sense of personal agency. Children with early trauma histories have an amorphous or underdeveloped sense of self. Like infants, they need constant reinforcement of a caregiver's awareness of them. With adequate repetition, a child can internalize a caregiver's awareness and transform it into self-awareness. School-aged children who lacked positive early attachment experiences benefit from classroom environments where teachers encourage children to notice and acknowledge positive attributes of one another. These activities serve a reparative function for children who need to develop greater self-awareness, while at the same time fostering a climate of belonging and respect.

Polling and other informal queries about children's preferences for simple things such as writing materials, taste in music, and snacks give children opportunities to define who they are in a safe and playful manner. Each time a teacher or peer references a child's personal preference, they provide the child with feedback that strengthens self-definition. Repeated

WHAT ADMINISTRATORS CAN DO

1. Create a school climate that fosters collaboration and bonding rather than hierarchical relationships.

2. Provide all staff with professional development training on brain-based behavior management techniques.

3. Provide opportunities to participate in wellness programs that include workshops on stress management and relaxation techniques.

4. Create a school climate in which children have easy access to adults in supportive roles. Encourage mentoring relationships, classroom meetings, and interns recruited from local graduate school programs in education, social work, and psychology to achieve this goal.

5. Foster a school climate where teachers are encouraged to collaborate with children in a manner that helps them regulate their emotions and maintain a comfortable level of arousal. Developmentally appropriate pacing and level of difficulty helps children stay involved and avoid "zoning out" or feeling overwhelmed. So do frequent check-ins and movement breaks.

6. Provide teachers with professional development concerning the need to include options for soothing sensory input in the positive behavioral support they make available to children. These include easy access to music and movement, as well as fidget toys, weighted blankets or vests, and a variety of textured materials.

7. Foster a school climate that builds children's capacity for optimism through schoolwide goal setting and public acknowledgment of positive outcomes.

8. Publicly acknowledge the contributions of those who go out of their way to help make school activities a success.

9. Provide staff with professional development training concerning the nature and intensity of traumatic memories.

10. Provide teachers with frequent opportunities to acquire the skills needed to manage their own internal state and avoid triggering reenactments of children's past traumas. Working effectively with traumatized children requires teachers to monitor their own reactions to student behaviors in order to remain objective, especially when de-escalating volatile behavior.

11. Approach children's behavior with curiosity rather than judgment. Ask "What were you thinking when you threw that block?" rather than saying, "Don't throw that block again."

12. Encourage teachers to show an unwavering and consistent interest in the children they are responsible for. Provide coverage as needed so that teachers can collaborate with mental health professionals on an as-needed basis to create appropriate interventions for specific children.

13. Partner with community agencies to sponsor mentorship programs for children who can benefit from individualized adult attention.

14. Eliminate grading policies that penalize children who do not complete homework or out-of-class projects.

15. Develop and implement schoolwide expectations of adult–child interactions that foster acceptance and respect. For example, use children's names when addressing them. Encourage staff and students to greet one another when they pass in the hallways. Display artwork that celebrates diversity and inclusion.

16. Use school songs, mottos, logos, and so forth to help children connect with their school as a home base where they belong.

often enough, this feedback enables children to construct a self-image that includes self-regulatory monitoring of their behavior.

IMPLICATIONS FOR EDUCATIONAL REFORM

Staff in trauma-sensitive schools focus on what Carol Lee refers to as "the developmental processes by which humans learn how to address the challenges of cultivating and sustaining a sense of well-being and competence, of nurturing interpersonal relationships . . . and navigating obstacles" (Lee, 2007, p. 222). Staff are "emotional detectives": rather than judging students, they try to understand them and help correct cognitive distortions that inhibit self-regulation.

Children's ability to self-regulate develops slowly and changes in response to environmental conditions. It is not unusual for regressions to occur in stressful situations. This is particularly true for children with early trauma histories. When something triggers a traumatic memory, the ability to cortically mediate the reaction is compromised. In other words, because these memories are sensory in nature, children cannot use thinking to control their reactions and are likely to express their discomfort physically.

WHAT TEACHERS CAN DO

1. Use eye contact, interest, and gesture matching to convey respect to children as well as a willingness to collaborate with them.

2. Replace authoritarian classroom management techniques with brain-based strategies that build a sense of collaboration and support.

3. Hold children to high expectations for performance and behavior paired with the scaffolds and accommodations children need to achieve them.

4. Provide children with opportunities to care for one another by providing a needed service or support.

5. Be emotionally available to children, supporting their efforts to manage their emotions and behavior.

6. Create a classroom environment that supports a dynamic relationship between the brain, mind, and body of both the students and teachers who participate in it.

7. Use observation to appraise children's inner states, and support their efforts at self-regulation based on your perception.

8. Use observation and active listening to establish positive relationships with children that allow them to feel safe and free to explore.

9. Provide positive behavioral supports such as physical proximity, choices about seating, visual templates, and developmentally appropriate pacing to help them maintain a comfortable level of arousal.

10. Provide children with easy access to soothing sensory input to help them self-regulate.

11. Provide children with opportunities to strengthen their prefrontal cortex through goal setting, choice making, and self-reflection.

12. Encourage children to notice and acknowledge the positive attributes of one another.

13. Create opportunities for children to build self-esteem by playing "status roles" within the classroom, such as line leader or flag holder.

14. Follow a consistent daily schedule to help children learn what to expect.

15. Engage children in serve and return exchanges to deal with their understanding of reciprocal relationships.

16. Provide children with opportunities to explore their interests through enrichment activities that broaden their experience and expose them to alternative ways of imagining a future.

A return to more cortically mediated behavior occurs most easily when children have opportunities to engage in behaviors that restore balance in the parts of the brain associated with sensory input. Examples include rhythmic movement, rocking, singing, drumming, sucking, and deep breathing. Providing access to a sensory diet that includes these types of activities is an example of how staff in trauma-sensitive schools serve as "co-regulators," helping children control their level of arousal and avoid impulsive, angry outbursts. With teacher support, children learn to recognize the first signs of heightened arousal and opt for a short period of rocking, drumming, or simply walking around the room until calm is restored and they are able to return to their schoolwork.

CONCLUSION

Children's attachment relationships affect every aspect of development, including genetic expression and neuroplasticity. Secure attachments encourage children's exploration of the environment and interest in learning new things. Patterns of insecure attachment have the opposite effect. Various types of economic, emotional, and epigenetic experiences alter the neural architecture of the brain in ways that limit children's ability to trust themselves or others. Positive attachment relationships with teachers help students compensate for early attachment failures. Positive experiences in school give them the confidence they need to explore new concepts and behavior. Within this protective environment, children are able to reshape their perceptions of themselves and others.

CHAPTER 4

Trauma's Effects on Children's Readiness to Learn

Confusion now hath made its masterpiece.

—Shakespeare

The detrimental effects of trauma on children's academic and social competence begin early. Disruptions in initial attachment relationships interfere with the development of representational thought—that is, the ability to use images and words to think about the internal and external world. It is the cognitive underpinning of empathy and language, and it is closely associated with memory, attention, and executive functioning.

This chapter explores how early trauma affects children's ability to form mental images of themselves and others. How this affects their development of empathy and representational thought is discussed as they relate to inferential reasoning, language development, and executive functioning.

THE DEVELOPMENT OF REPRESENTATIONAL THOUGHT

The development of representational thought begins with children's sensory motor exploration of their environment, progresses to mental images of nonverbal concepts, and eventually progresses to words. It reflects the dual capacity of the brain to think symbolically and effectively discriminate between the self and others.

Sensory Motor Development

At birth children cannot distinguish a self from their sensations. Only as they interact with caregivers do they learn that they are more than what they feel. They become aware of the effect their behavior has on others. Crying signals a response from the caregiver that relieves hunger or discomfort.

44

Smiling and cooing are reciprocated by similar expressions and vocalizations from others. Exploration of the environment reveals new sensations and builds infants' awareness of their ability to repeat pleasurable experiences and avoid those found distasteful. Connections are made between familiar objects and the sensations they connote through playful exchanges with loving caregivers. So when a child sees a favorite blanket, he anticipates the pleasure of its soft texture and cozy warmth. When he sees his bottle, he gets excited because he knows it is time to eat. The child is thinking symbolically, using representational thought for the first time.

It is not long before the child learns to use gestures or other nonverbal communication to convey what he wants. He learns to interpret the nonverbal communication of others: his mother's smile or frown, or the direct eye contact of a desired playmate. This marks an important milestone in the development of representational thought. The child is not just using symbols to communicate; he is learning to discriminate between himself and others who have thoughts and feelings of their own. With the acquisition of language, the child is able to express his own thoughts and feelings, and to use others' verbal and nonverbal communication to judge their intention and predict their behavior.

Early trauma and attachment failures derail these developmental changes in a variety of ways. Blurred parental boundaries characterize the insecure attachment that results from their own childhood trauma. Caregivers cannot distinguish between parents' needs and those of their children. This limits their ability to provide for children's needs in a manner that promotes self-differentiation and emotional regulation.

Becoming Aware of the Thoughts of Others

Children's verbal ability and semantic memory develop simultaneously. Together they enable children to hold internal images of people, objects, and events in their minds even when these are no longer present. This sense of object permanence allows children to think about others in an abstract manner, attributing motivations and feelings to their behavior.

As children become more aware of others as separate individuals with thoughts and intentions of their own, they learn to see situations from other people's points of view. They learn to pick up on what others are thinking, and become more adept at anticipating another's behavior based on prior experiences. They learn to include representations of the thoughts and feelings of others in their own thinking and realize that others do likewise. These new insights into others' mental states increase children's ability to engage in shared narratives and enjoy the company of their peers.

Repeated experiences of unpredictable, inconsistent caregiving interfere with children's acquisition of object permanence. Their inability to understand that persons or objects still exist when out of sight, or that they themselves exist in the minds of others, diminishes their capacity for representational thought (Craig, 2001; van der Kolk, 2005). Lack of insight into the thoughts and feelings of others makes children insensitive to someone else's needs and incapable of sharing their perspective.

Developing Empathy

Empathy flows from the ability to recognize and share another's emotional state (Hastings, Zahn-Waxler, & McShane, 2006). It is traditionally assumed that some children are just more sensitive or intuitive than others. It is in their nature to be altruistic and kind. Science now shows that there is much more to it.

Empathy is shaped by an interaction of environmental and biological processes that occur over the course of development. It is characterized by both affective and cognitive components. The affective component enables children's ability to match or join in the affective experiences of another. The cognitive component helps them move beyond egocentrism to the realization that others have their own experiences. Eventually, they learn to interpret the thoughts and feelings of others.

The development of both the affective and cognitive aspects of empathy occurs within children's early attachment relationships. In this context, they experience feelings of connection to the caregiver, as well as episodes of social rejection. In secure attachment relationships, episodes of rejecting behavior are quickly repaired by the caregiver. Reparation does not occur in insecure or disorganized attachment relationships. As a result, children learn to expect to be rejected by others.

In either case, these experiences link the circuits in the brain responsible for social behavior and physical pain. These connect with the circuitry that enables children to discriminate between themselves and others. The interactions between these circuits are the basis for empathic behavior.

There is some debate as to how these neural circuits interact with one another to produce empathic thought and behaviors. Simulation theory (Rameson & Lieberman, 2009) favors an experiential model. Proponents argue that children use their own experiences with pain and self-soothing as a model for what others need in similar situations. When others have been a source of comfort to them, they are motivated to reach out to others to reduce their distress.

This position is defended by the fact that the same neural structures appear to be recruited when one is personally experiencing something or observing another in the same circumstances.

By contrast, theory-of-mind advocates take a more cognitive approach. They argue that empathic connection is the result of children's ability to think about the contents of another's mind, and adjust their behavior to their perception of how they are feeling. Mediated by the medial prefrontal cortex, empathy involves a more conscious decision about how to behave toward another. Like simulation theory, the choice of how to connect to the other is limited by children's own experiences.

Early childhood trauma interferes with the development of empathy. As a result, many children with early trauma histories are less inclined than peers to notice or seek to alleviate the distress of others. This is due in part to their blunted affect, which both limits awareness of their own discomfort and compromises their ability to self-soothe. On the other hand, some traumatized children can appear overly empathic, as if trying to alleviate their own pain by being overly solicitous of others.

The effects of trauma on the medial prefrontal cortex also play a role. Traumatized children have a limited ability to interpret the thoughts and feelings of others. They are often viewed as socially inept, behaving in a manner not unlike some children with Asperger's syndrome. Their difficulty inferring another's feelings or intentions makes it difficult for others to predict how they will think or act. This leads to errors in social cognition, as well as difficulty with inferential comprehension in reading and math.

THE EFFECTS OF EARLY TRAUMA ON LANGUAGE DEVELOPMENT

Language functions as a bridge between children's internal and external worlds. It helps children monitor their behavior, communicate with those around them, and explore the world of ideas. Early trauma threatens all aspects of language development. Lack of consistency in caregiving relationships reduces the ability of children to use self-talk to monitor behavior and anticipate what comes next in everyday routines. The same activities either do not happen at all or happen at random times of the day, making it hard to anticipate their occurrence. Communication with others is difficult when children's safety needs interfere with their ability to pay attention to what is being said. Limited vocabulary makes exploration of ideas and self-expression less likely to occur.

The neural architecture of language is embedded in a complex system of large-scale connectivity with other regions of the brain, including the prefrontal cortex, the hippocampus, the amygdala, and the corpus callosum. These circuits develop within the context of children's early caregiving relationships. When these relationships are developmentally appropriate and supportive, caregivers help children bring meaning to experiences by labeling them and using words to place them in the context of past, present, and future. Children learn to translate symbolic representations into mental images of what they signify.

They do this by internalizing the process of using language to "talk to themselves." This self-talk is an integral component of self-regulation and lays the foundation for higher-order thinking and problem solving.

Children whose early experiences are marred by trauma often lack the ability to use language in this manner. This is due in part to the nonverbal aspects of traumatic experience. Children are unable to put words to feelings. Instead, the nonverbal right hemisphere signals through gestures, facial expression, tone of voice, and behavior that something is wrong. These wordless experiences cannot be sufficiently integrated into consciousness, nor will they rest quietly. Instead, "the survivor is haunted by an unnarrated past" (Bloom & Farragher, 2011, p. 113).

Language and the Emergent Self

The development of a coherent sense of self depends to a large extent on children's internalized speech, or self-talk. In secure attachment relationships, caregivers spend a lot of time each day talking to children about everyday activities and routines. They reminisce about things they enjoyed doing or people they were happy to see. They help children anticipate what is happening in the near future and what preparations need to be made. They use words to talk about children's behavior, and make suggestions if need be about how to change what they are doing to be more successful in achieving their goals. With enough practice, children eventually continue this dialogue with themselves, using it to monitor their behavior and prepare for upcoming events.

When parents engage children in this type of dialogue, they increase the capacity to learn by providing a large vocabulary, teaching them to use language to monitor their behavior, and encouraging them to think in a sequential manner that positions events in the past, present, or future. This fosters a coherent sense of self, as well as the ability to observe the same experience from various perspectives.

The disruptive nature of interpersonal trauma inhibits the development of these important skills. Caregivers who are incapable of forming secure

Figure 4.1. Language Centers of Brain

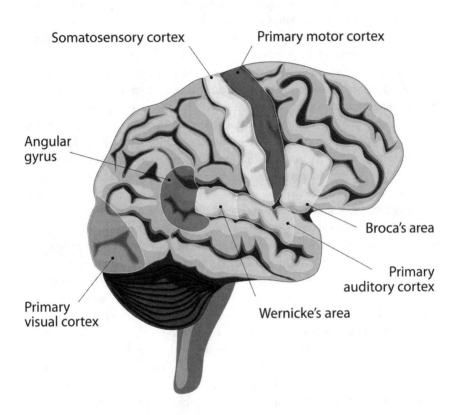

attachments seldom engage children in the ongoing collaboration required for the development of internal language. As a result, children whose attachment pattern is avoidant, resistant, or disorganized show deficits in areas of linear sequential thought and perspective taking. They are impulsive and generally lack strong self-monitoring skills. Their limited exposure to meaningful conversations with adults results in depressed vocabulary scores, while memories of their "unnarrated past" produce an incoherent and confused sense of self (Bloom & Farragher, 2011, p. 113).

Language and Information Exchange

Maltreatment in early childhood significantly affects the neural pathways that link the language centers of the left and right hemispheres—specifically the Broca's area located in the inferior frontal cortex and the Wernicke's area located in the superior temporal gyrus (see Figure 4.1).

Neurons in the Broca's area are responsible for the production of speech sounds and expressive language. This area formulates and understands the meaning of words and sentences. It is an area of the brain that is particularly sensitive to stress. Cortisol and other hormones produced by stress inhibit activity in the area, literally leaving one "at a loss for words."

The close relationship between anxiety and Broca's area activity has serious implications for children with early trauma histories. Their chronic state of heightened arousal makes it difficult for them to express themselves or use language for problem solving, even when they have age-appropriate vocabulary at their command. It is not uncommon for them to remain speechless when asked for information or justification for their behavior. Their silence is often judged to be sullen or defiant, when it is simply a phys-iological reaction to stress.

Similarly, heightened anxiety makes it difficult for new information to be stored in the Broca's area or retrieved easily in a test situation. This explains why children with early trauma histories benefit more from multisensory in-struction than a more traditional lecture format. A multisensory approach allows for storage and retrieval in areas of the brain less sensitive to stress.

Neurons in the Wernicke's area interpret the emotional connotation of what is being said. This area of the superior temporal gyrus is responsi-ble for interpreting the speaker's facial cues. It develops prior to speech as the infant attunes to the melody, intonation, and prosody of the caregiver's voice (Bogolepova & Malofeeva, 2001). These become the lens through which children interpret the nonverbal aspects of all future communication. As such they become a barometer of the speaker's mood, warning the child of any potential threat.

These implicit memories exert considerable influence on children's abil-ity to pay attention to what is being said to them and act on the information being conveyed. Children with early trauma histories easily miss the content of what is being said to them because their attention is focused on subtle changes in the speaker's facial expression or tone of voice that may signal danger. They are also prone to misattributions of negativity in the nonverbal communication of adults and peers (Rude, Wenglaff, Gibbs, Vane, & Whit-ney, 2002). These misperceptions make it difficult for maltreated children to use language for information exchange, or to correctly interpret social situations and adjust their behavior accordingly.

Language and Interpersonal Relationships

The communication required to form and sustain interpersonal relation-ships relies on the integration of the language centers of the left and right hemispheres (see Figure 4.2).

Figure 4.2. Brain Hemispheres and Corpus Callosum

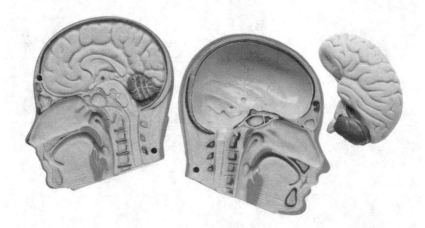

In normal development, this occurs through ongoing information exchange across the corpus callosum, a thick cable of nerve fiber that connects the two sides of the brain. This transfer of information across hemispheres allows for the integration of words and emotions. The better integrated the brain's hemispheres become, the more likely it is that children acquire the bilateral coherence necessary for self-reflection and higher-order thinking.

Early trauma interferes with this process in several ways. The volume of the corpus callosum in children who are maltreated is lower than that of their peers (D'Andrea, Ford, Stolbach, Spinazzola, & van der Kolk, 2012; Teicher, Dumont, Ito, Vaituzis, Giedd & Andersen, 2004). They have difficulty integrating the verbal and nonverbal aspects of communication, making it difficult for them to engage in conversation. They frequently misinterpret body language and facial cues, attributing negative intent to benign feedback from others. Spontaneous speech is difficult for them, limiting their ability to communicate subjective experiences to others.

Integration of the left and right hemispheres is further compromised by the fact that trauma triggers activate memories in the right hemisphere while deactivating the executive functioning of the left. This makes it difficult for children to organize experiences into sequential steps or translate shifting feelings and perceptions into words (van der Kolk, 2014). Their ability to grasp the consequences of their behavior is limited, as well as their ability to create coherent plans for the future. As a result, peers view them as unpredictable playmates who are unaware of the social rules that help form and sustain friendships. Incapable of contingent, collaborative communication, children with early trauma histories are isolated or rejected by peers.

Figure 4.3. Neural Pathway, Synapse

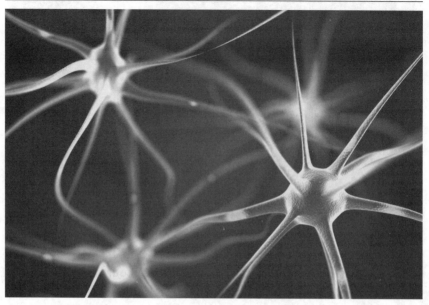

THE EFFECTS OF TRAUMA ON CHILDREN'S ATTENTION, MEMORY, AND EXECUTIVE FUNCTION

Attention, memory, and executive function are interwoven in a complex system of neural networks that is crucial to the learning process. Early childhood trauma has a domino effect that causes a pervasive pattern of attention, memory, and executive function deficits.

Attention

The brain develops in a use-dependent manner that relies to a great extent on children's early environment. Interactions with caregivers prime the brain to expect certain experiences, which it then prepares for by forming an anticipatory set of neural pathways or synapses ready to respond (see Figure 4.3).

Frequent stimulation strengthens these pathways, thereby producing an automatic reaction. Pathways that are left unattended are eventually discarded. This process of creating, strengthening, and discarding synapses allows the brain to adapt to its unique surroundings.

The use-dependent nature of the brain, along with the relational context in which it develops, biases children's attention toward familiar experiences and relationships. Opportunities to explore their surroundings within the safety of a secure attachment relationship prepare children to attend to stimulating activities and to show an interest in those around them.

Children living with chronic stress or trauma are wired to respond to threatening or dangerous situations. Although it is possible for them to develop neural pathways receptive to exploration and intellectual curiosity, their day-to-day experiences direct their attention elsewhere. Their attention bias is toward survival. It follows them into classrooms, where it limits their ability to participate in classroom activities that require a willingness to engage in novel or risk-taking behaviors.

The hypervigilance or survival bias of traumatized children makes them particularly sensitive to perceptions of threat, causing frequent deactivation of the left hemisphere. Their reflexive tendency to downshift to a fight, flight, or freeze mentality derails their attention. This makes it difficult for them to focus within a classroom environment where activities require an ability to think sequentially, understand causal relationships, and concentrate on the content being conveyed. Their attention is frequently directed toward the nonverbal behaviors of others, which they are prone to interpret as negative or rejecting.

Children living in adverse circumstances are often more anxious than their peers. In some cases the anxiety stems from concerns about family members or worries about housing, food shortages, and other responsibilities that exceed their ability to cope. Others have a high startle, and overreact to sudden changes in the environment. Some children's anxiety is so high that they use ritualistic behaviors to try to control it and self-soothe. In any case, anxiety is distracting and interferes with children's ability to focus and pay attention. This negatively affects what they learn, as well as the degree of interest they bring to activities with peers.

Memory

Memories are the organizational framework for children's development (Davis & Logie, 1993). Implicit memories are formed in infancy and are for the most part nonverbal. They include memories of reflexive behaviors and conditioned responses that unconsciously are acted upon. Unarticulated feelings about early attachment experiences are also stored unconsciously as implicit memories. These exert a powerful influence on relationships and behavior. They are so closely aligned with one's self-definition that they are seldom experienced "as anything other than the self" (Cozolino, 2013, p. 227).

Children whose early attachment relationships are marred by abuse or neglect are likely to have implicit memories of rejection, fear, and self-hatred that limit their ability to form positive relationships with teachers or peers. Coupled with poor regulatory control, these unconscious memories can result in aggressive, self-destructive behaviors that are difficult to manage or explain. Left unattended, they pose a real threat to children's ability to achieve academic or social mastery.

Explicit memories emerge when children are around 2 years old (Siegler, 1998). They are language based and can be consciously recalled. Episodic memories are autobiographical in nature, providing a snapshot of what is important in someone's life. Semantic memories are less personal but include all the knowledge available for recollection. Together, they create access to the internal and external world through the use of intentional recollection (Gross, 2013).

Explicit memories depend on conceptually driven top-down processing of new information or experiences. Their formation always depends on a recognition system that reorganizes and stores the new data with information that appears related. Explicit memory formation relies on prior knowledge, as well as multiple opportunities to use or manipulate the new experiences.

Executive Function

The prefrontal cortex represents the area of the brain that is responsible for the conscious regulation of thought, emotion, and behavior (see Figure 4.4).

It develops slowly and is eventually capable of controlling the lower brain in a manner that allows the translation of knowledge into action. Sometimes referred to as the brain's "executive director," the prefrontal cortex is responsible for organizing thoughts and ideas, planning, strategizing, and self-monitoring—in other words, learning to use one's brain advantageously. It accomplishes these tasks primarily through the executive functions of inhibitory control, working memory, and cognitive flexibility. While genes provide the blueprint for executive functioning, the early environment and relationships to which children are exposed affect how the capacity develops. The environment's ability to encourage the expression of qualities associated with academic mastery is a better predictor of school success than intelligence alone.

Inhibitory Control. Inhibitory control involves two important aspects of goal-oriented behavior: delayed gratification and distraction suppression. A well-known example of delayed gratification is the famous "marshmallow

Figure 4.4. Prefrontal Cortex

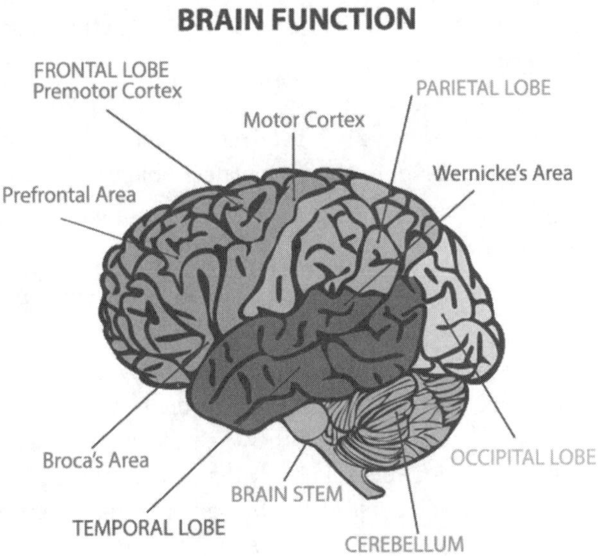

BRAIN FUNCTION

FRONTAL LOBE
Premotor Cortex

Motor Cortex

PARIETAL LOBE

Wernicke's Area

Prefrontal Area

Broca's Area

BRAIN STEM

OCCIPITAL LOBE

TEMPORAL LOBE

CEREBELLUM

test," in which 4-year-old children are given two marshmallows and told to wait until the examiner comes back in the room to eat them. If necessary, they can push a buzzer to shorten the wait time, but the reward will be cut in half. They will receive only one marshmallow (Mischel, Ebbesen, & Raskoff Zeiss, 1972). The test measures children's ability to control their impulses to achieve a desired goal. Children who were able to endure the wait were later shown to have greater success at school than their peers.

Distraction suppression involves the ability to remain focused on a desired target by ignoring or suppressing the urge to pay attention to irrelevant information. Distraction suppression is most easily achieved by children who have prior experience with similar tasks, as well as strong discrimination and scanning skills. Both aspects of inhibitory control are prominent corollaries of early math and reading ability (Blair & Razza, 2007).

Working Memory. Working memory is a neural circuit consisting of the cortex, the hippocampus, and the para-hippocampal areas of the brain. It is what one is thinking about when learning something new. Working memory briefly stores new information as it is processed and eventually stored in long-term memory. The cortex selects what is to be remembered. The hippocampus and para-hippocampal areas encode the information, and then retrieve related long-term memories into which they simultaneously

WHAT ADMINISTRATORS CAN DO

1. Cultivate relationships with children that emphasize their unique contribution to the school community.

2. Hold schoolwide debates and write-in campaigns that help children learn to generate alternative perspectives on schoolwide topics of interest and alternative solutions to schoolwide problems.

3. Treat parents and teachers in the empathic manner you want them to use with children.

4. Enact discipline policies that support children's efforts to repair any harm that their misbehavior causes others.

5. Hold two short assemblies each week. On Monday review upcoming events and needed preparations. Ask for student volunteers. On Friday, summarize what happened during the week, citing clear successes and things that could be improved. Publicly thank student participants. This type of goal setting and public acknowledgment strengthens children's sense of personal agency and executive functioning.

6. Provide teachers with professional development training focused on strategies that promote a whole brain approach to learning. Encourage them to include multisensory activities for all instruction. Eric Jensen (2013) and Marilee Sprenger (2013) are two good resources for finding creative brain-based strategies.

7. Work with children to construct a timeline of the school year. Post it in the school's main corridor and update it weekly with pictures and text describing events of the week.

8. Seek out opportunities to help children recognize the beneficial consequences of their behavior. Use pictures and scripted language to underscore the relationship. This helps children grasp the causal effects of their behavior within the context of a safe, positive interaction.

9. Closely monitor the school environment to ensure that it provides children and staff with the physical, emotional, and social safety needed to learn and grow. Conduct "safety audits" to prevent unsafe practices from slipping through the cracks.

10. Keep video scrapbooks of school activities and routines. Play them on monitors in the hallways and cafeteria to foster a sense of community and a positive school spirit.

11. Collaborate with children to set schoolwide goals. Model goal-directed behaviors. Publicize goal attainment through local newspapers, school websites, and parent newsletters.

12. Create your own "innovation nation" (https://www.thehenryford.org/
    innovationnation). Organize teams of students who compete with one
    another to find new solutions to old problems faced by other children
    their age.

integrate the newly acquired information (Lovallo, 2005). Thus the brain is able to expand its understanding of a topic by embedding new data into an existing framework.

The reduced hippocampal volume characteristic of children with early trauma histories explains some of their difficulty with working memory (Teicher, Anderson, & Polcari, 2012). They have greater difficulty than peers when making associations between relevant stimuli or integrating new information into existing schemas. Their difficulty in achieving automaticity in basic skills further decreases the capacity of their working memories by requiring them to consciously think through basic skills that peers can apply automatically.

Cognitive Flexibility. Cognitive flexibility is the aspect of executive functioning that facilitates creative problem solving. It enables children to approach issues from different perspectives or points of view. It inspires divergent thinking and the ability to "think outside the box." It encourages learners to continually look for new and better ways of reaching goals and achieving what they set out to do.

Although children with early trauma history find all aspects of executive functioning difficult, cognitive flexibility may be their greatest challenge. By its very nature, trauma limits children's ability to change the way they think about things, especially how they think about themselves or adults who try to help them. The tracks of self-hatred and mistrust run deep, and children trip on them often. Their perseveration on the past limits their ability to move beyond it. Compulsive repetitions of traumatic interactions with adults sap the energy needed to take advantage of new opportunities. Intrusive memories of harmful events are a constant reminder to remain focused on survival rather than taking the risk to try something new.

IMPLICATIONS FOR EDUCATIONAL REFORM

The pervasive nature of the effects of early trauma on children's readiness to learn underscores the need to view children's academic and social behavior through a trauma-sensitive lens. Integrating this perspective into reform

What Teachers Can Do

1. Use charades and pantomime to foster children's awareness of body language and the meanings it conveys.

2. Engage children in literacy activities that encourage them to write alternative endings, and discuss text from the perspectives of different characters.

3. Approach children's problems with empathy and a willingness to support their efforts to find a solution

4. Help children repair any damage they do to another's feelings or reputation. Initiate reparative behavior for any perceived disrespect you may have shown a child.

5. Integrate relationship building activities into everyday classroom routines.

6. Engage children in purposeful conversations that encourage them to explore their interests and plan for the future.

7. Use a consistent cue and familiar format to help children pay attention to instructional content or information exchange. For example, use a prop such as a magic wand or megaphone to signal that what comes next is important content that requires children's undivided attention. Chunk the information into age appropriate segments (one minute for each year of the groups chronological age), and follow it up with an immediate activity that reinforces what is said.

8. Provide children with scaffolds such as scripts, conversation starters, and role-playing to build their capacity to use language to create relationships with peers.

9. Design instruction in a manner that guarantees multiple presentations of the same content using a variety of modalities to develop and strengthen children's neural pathways.

10. Use rituals and predictable routines to create a sense of familiarity in the classroom.

11. Design instruction so that children have multiple opportunities to immediately apply new information so that it can be remembered more easily.

12. Provide students with accommodations like calculators and spell-check to compensate for deficits in automaticity so they have more working memory available for higher-order thinking.

efforts has the potential to explain the persistence of learning problems in children who do not benefit from traditional interventions.

The emotional dysregulation and lack of personal agency experienced by so many traumatized children requires a conscious commitment on the part of administrators and teachers to cultivate students' self-awareness and higher-order thinking. With enough repetition, these experiences can help children acquire the tools needed to take control of their thinking and behavior.

CONCLUSION

Early trauma affects every aspect of children's cognitive development: representational thought, language, memory, attention, and executive functioning. As a result, children with histories of adversity face significant disadvantages in meeting the academic and social demands of school. Aware of this, staff in trauma-sensitive schools integrate foundational skill development into everyday activities and routines. Efforts to reduce children's survival bias include frequent reassurances and consistent use of established routines. Together, these efforts help children exert greater control over their attention and eventually result in an increased capacity for executive functioning.

CHAPTER 5

Retooling the Teacher's Role in Trauma-Sensitive Schools

One cannot underestimate the therapeutic impact of a caring teacher.

—*Bruce Perry and Christine Ludy-Dobson*

The teacher's role in a trauma-sensitive school is to integrate what we now know of children's neurodevelopment into classroom practice to help students overcome trauma-related challenges. Primary emphasis is placed on instructional design, implementation of a tiered system of support for children's self-regulation, and collaborative partnerships with children that provide them with the coaching they need to make good choices and avoid self-destructive behaviors. Teachers do not have to mention trauma to be trauma-sensitive. They do have to engage children in noncoercive ways. The use of threats or authoritarian expectations is likely to trigger the fight, flight, or freeze reaction in traumatized children and limit their ability to learn.

This chapter presents an in-depth discussion of two instructional designs that are particularly advantageous to children with trauma histories. Both emphasize teachers' use of ongoing formative assessment, which helps children acquire the self-awareness they lack as a result of early traumatizing experiences. A tiered intervention model for use within a trauma-sensitive school is described, as well as the benefits of collaborative teacher–student partnerships. Strategies for using these partnerships to buffer stress, prevent reenactments, and foster personal agency are provided.

DESIGNING TRAUMA-SENSITIVE INSTRUCTION

Instructional design in a trauma-sensitive school makes use of current research on children's neurodevelopment. Ongoing formative assessment helps teachers differentiate instruction in a manner that is responsive to children's needs and preferences. Teachers then work with the brain's plasticity to optimize children's capacity for higher-order thinking and executive functioning.

Neurodevelopment and Instructional Best Practices

Magnetic resonance imaging (MRI) provides important insights into the neural processes that organize children's cognition. These data provide a framework for teachers to develop and sustain classroom environments that work with the brain's plasticity or adaptability to enhance children's development. These enriching practices begin with the teacher's ability to foster positive relationships and extend to physical aspects and emotional tone of the learning environment.

There is no question that teachers can offer children the opportunity to reverse earlier attachment failures. To be successful in this role, they need to be knowledgeable about how the attachment process works and capable of understanding the emotions that result in disruptive or hostile behaviors. Equipped with these competencies, teachers can collaborate with children and help them to acquire the control needed to regulate their feelings and behavior.

Teachers are most successful with traumatized children when they are able to establish themselves as a source of comfort and a secure base for exploration and learning. They establish this sense of connection by creating a relationship that reflects a balance of support and opportunity. They build children's self-esteem by holding them to high expectations while providing the necessary scaffolds to guarantee success. The focus is on cultivating a sense of well-being and competence through repeated experiences of acceptance and care (Green, 2014). With enough support, children learn how to navigate around obstacles and display adequate persistence in the face of difficulty.

As children begin to experience academic success, it is important for teachers to recognize their role as "brain builders." Committed to using neuroplasticity to help children achieve their highest potential, they set clear goals about the higher-order thinking skills they want children to acquire. They then design instructional activities that expose children to an appropriate level of neurodevelopmental demand, with scaffolding provided as needed.

This neurodevelopmental model of instruction reflects two important shifts in teacher performance. The first involves expanding the focus of ongoing assessment to include an evaluation of the power of particular activities to achieve neurodevelopmental goals. The second consists of

Figure 5.1. Dendrite Mass

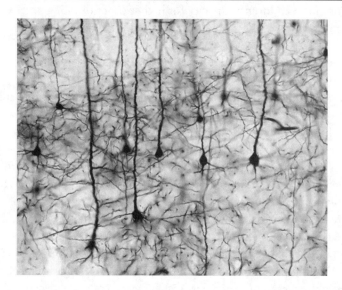

differentiating instruction in a manner that allows children to meet content expectations using a variety of processing skills: auditory, visual, and motor.

Children build their capacity for higher-order thinking and cognitive control within safe, comfortable environments. Protection from outside threats nourishes the brain's inherent curiosity. Within this context the teacher's role is transformational, expanding children's dendrite mass (see Figure 5.1) by helping them make new connections to prior knowledge.

Neural networks are strengthened by use of an instructional format that gives children frequent opportunities to do something with what they are learning—talk about it with a peer, complete a hands-on activity, or draw a picture symbolizing what they have learned. "Think-Pair-Share," Microsoft PowerPoint presentations, and interactive note taking are familiar strategies that can be used to provide opportunities for immediate reinforcement. Each facilitates storage in long-term memory, helping to "cement" the new information onto existing neural structures.

Customizing Instruction

Trauma-sensitive schools differentiate instruction using the principles of universal design for learning (UDL). First developed to ensure equal access for children with disabilities, these principles emphasize the need to design instruction in a manner that is flexible enough that it can be customized and adjusted to meet individual needs. Consideration is given to the three primary neural networks associated with learning: the recognition network, which is the "what" of learning; the strategic network, which is the "how" of learning; and the affective network, which the "why" of learning (CAST, 2011). Assuming that learning differences exist in any group, instruction is designed in such a manner that there are multiple routes of access to each network.

Recognition Network. The *recognition network* consists of the mechanisms by which children gather facts and categorize them. When the same information and content are available in multiple modalities, children tend to select the one they are most comfortable with. This increases the speed with which they can recognize patterns and efficiently categorize new information.

Children with early trauma histories share the need for presentation of material in multiple modalities. They also require accommodations to unique characteristics of their language processing. These include their tendency to focus on the relational aspects of language. Traumatized children often miss important information or content because they pay more attention to the teacher's face and body language than to what is being said. They struggle with spontaneous speech and have difficulty responding to direct questions. Teachers need to be aware of these effects of trauma so that when they differentiate the "what" of instruction, they include accommodations to these distinct learning characteristics.

Strategic Network. The *strategic network* involves how children plan and perform tasks, and how they organize and express ideas. As such, it taps into the quality of children's executive function. This is an area of neurodevelopment that is seriously compromised in children with early trauma histories. Their chronic state of hyperarousal interferes with their ability to pay attention, as well as their working memory. Their learning style is characterized by impulsive trial and error rather than planning and self-reflection. They are children who "act and then think" (van der Kolk, 2001), who give up easily in the face of new or challenging tasks.

Teachers build the capacity of these children to think strategically when they integrate appropriate scaffolding into classroom tasks. Scaffolding is used to both reduce the amount of working memory used to manage low-level skills such as computation or keyboarding, and to increase student use of higher-level executive functions such as goal setting and performance monitoring.

Scaffolding to manage low-level skills includes accommodations that provide easy access to baseline information that students need to participate in higher-order thinking activities. Tools such as word banks, number lines, calculators, and predictive software increase the amount of working memory available for more complex problem solving.

Explicit instruction and close teacher–student collaboration are required to develop children's higher-level executive functions. Teaching children to set goals requires building their capacity to understand basic concepts. Early trauma and/or attachment failures interfere with children's understanding of sequence, prediction and estimation, and time. Traumatized children experience events as random, uncontrollable, and unrelated to what has occurred in the past. They need help understanding the relationship between effort and outcome. They live in the moment and find it difficult to project a future where they can control what happens to them.

Meaningful scaffolds include teacher modeling of goal-setting behaviors, as well as close collaboration with students as they create plans to meet personal goals. These include explicit feedback that is provided in a timely, informative manner, in addition to opportunities for children to reflect on their progress and performance. Consistent implementation of these types of scaffolds helps strengthen the prefrontal cortex, making children's executive functioning more effective and automatic.

Affective Network. The *affective network* involves knowing how to attract children's attention, engage their interests, and sustain their effort. It is a neural network that relies on teachers' willingness to engage children in an ongoing dialogue about how to design instruction in a manner that is both interesting to them and capable of sustaining their attention and effort. Together, ongoing formative assessments of both the purpose and process of instruction, as well as its outcomes, create a dynamic feedback loop between teachers and students in which both have a voice. Stagnant repetition of one-size-fits-all lesson plans is replaced with plans that reflect the unique experiences of one teacher and one group of students.

Such close collaboration with teachers is conducive to helping children with early trauma histories learn. For perhaps the first time, children know an adult is interested in them and willing to change to accommodate their needs.

This sense of connection places teachers in a unique position to help traumatized children. It helps children replace their innate sense of despair with optimism about their future. This change of perspective is strengthened each time teachers provide children with opportunities to learn about who they are and what they are capable of doing. Examples include giving children positive feedback about their personal attributes, such as offering to help a classmate catch up with their work. Specific praise about the effort children expend working on difficult tasks makes children more aware of their capacity for persistence and effortful control. Choice making is another way to foster this process of self-differentiation, especially when time is spent discussing whether the choices made help students achieve their personal goals. Staff in trauma-sensitive schools encourage children to make choices about how specific learning or behavioral objectives will be met; what tools will be used; and what, if any, support will be needed. Encouraging this level of autonomy increases classroom safety by giving children a voice in decisions that affect their lives (Green, 2014).

Safety is further enhanced by use of predictable classroom routines, calendars, charts, and visual timers that help children know what to do and how to do it. Alerts and previews prepare children for changes in activities or schedule, and help them anticipate what might happen during unusual or novel events.

Even within the context of a safe learning environment, children with early trauma histories require sustained apprenticeships to acquire age-appropriate self-regulatory behaviors. As they become more aware of their reactivity and internal state, continued support is needed to develop adaptive strategies for managing and directing their emotional states. These strategies typically center on coping with the anxiety caused by external triggers or internal rumination about events over which they have no control. Once acquired, the strategies allow children to direct their attention to classroom instruction and stay involved.

Dialogic Teaching

Dialogic teaching uses the power of conversation and dialogue to extend children's thinking and increase their understanding of things that they are learning. Children are introduced to different types of conversations, or "talk," that are used in different environments and for different purposes—talk for everyday life, learning talk, teaching talk, and language used for classroom organization. Each adheres to principles that promote collaborative, reciprocal relationships. Once in school, children quickly learn that teaching talk is often sprinkled with indirect requests that are meant to be obeyed, as, for example, "Would you please come to the reading table now?" Similar indirect requests, when used in everyday talk, do involve an actual choice, as in "Would you like to take a walk with me?" This is not the case when these questions are poised within a classroom context.

Children with early trauma histories are often deprived of language-rich home environments. Their parents spend little time talking to them. They do not engage in conversations about ideas. Time is not devoted to helping children articulate their opinions or to sharing hopes and dreams for the future.

Dialogic teaching provides new opportunities for children to explore how language can be used to explore other people's ideas. This helps children expand their ability to use representational thought, a skill that is critical to the development of both empathy and inferential comprehension (Johnston, 2012).

Another benefit of dialogic teaching is its use of questions that invite children to create new stories about themselves. The teacher's question "How did you . . . ?" helps children link their actions to positive outcomes for themselves and others. With enough practice, children are able to re-write their explanatory narrative.

IMPLEMENTATION OF A TIERED SYSTEM OF SUPPORT

The tiered approach to intervention employed in trauma-sensitive schools is unlike traditional service delivery models that require either special education eligibility and/or psychiatric diagnosis. Instead, trauma-sensitive schools rely on a public health model that uses risk assessment to determine needed supports. Risk factors such as poverty, recent life adjustments, ACEs, trauma history, and emotional and/or behavioral concerns determine the type and intensity of the supports provided. Approximately 85% of children function well with the support provided at Tier 1. Supports at Tier 1 are universal in nature and reflect sustained implementation of educational best practices, such as instruction at children's readiness level, positive behavioral supports, and use of developmentally appropriate language and pacing of instruction. The remaining 15% may need more targeted or intense Tier 2 and Tier 3 interventions. Tier 2 support is usually provided in small groups within the classroom. Interventions are provided by either the classroom teacher or an educational specialist knowledgeable in the area where additional support is required. Tier 2 interventions are usually skill based. Common examples include stress management and social skills. Tier 3 support is typically provided in an area outside the classroom by an educational specialist other than a classroom teacher. The ratio is 1:1 or 1:2, and intervention occurs daily for a short period of time. Tier 3 assistance is sometimes needed for children who are trying to manage an emotional crisis

Figure 5.2. Brain Stem and Midbrain

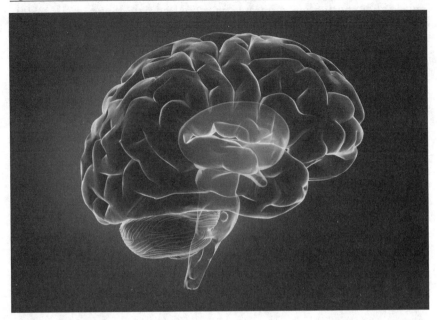

such as the death of a parent or a foster care placement. Any child can access the support available at each tier, depending on the child's life circumstances or instructional needs at any given time.

Tiered Interventions and the Hierarchical Development of the Brain

Use of tiered interventions provides trauma-sensitive schools with a flexible framework in which to assist children to regulate their own arousal by relating to them where they are developmentally and by reasoning with them at that level. Movement between tiers occurs as children's circumstances change, or as they become more capable of monitoring their behavior and regulating their emotions.

As children mature, they increase the frequency with which they use higher functioning areas of the brain to solve problems and work through frustration. Trauma alters this developing capacity by causing higher-than-normal levels of activity in the lower brain (the brain stem and midbrain; see Figure 5.2).

As a result, children with trauma histories have more difficulty using their higher brain to moderate reactive responses or to inhibit impulsive or aggressive behavior (Perry, 1997).

Tier 1 Interventions. Tier 1 interventions are traditionally referred to as universal supports that permeate the school climate (Sugai et al., 2000). They reflect expectations agreed upon by school staff and ensure that all children have access to a safe, caring learning environment. Because trauma-sensitive schools recognize that at any given time approximately 40% of their student population may have trauma histories, they are careful to anticipate unpredictable changes in student mood or behavior. Universal supports include staff capable of taking over when children's coping skills are inadequate to meet the challenge or deal with frustration. Examples include increasing a teacher's physical proximity in a manner that conveys comfort or support, redirecting a child's attention away from a frustrating task to something more pleasurable, or giving students ample time to transition from one activity to another.

The goal of Tier 1 interventions is to provide children with direct instruction on competencies associated with good mental health. These include self-awareness, self-management, social awareness, relationship skills, and responsible problem solving (Collaborative for Academic, Social, and Emotional Learning, 2004). Opportunities to learn and practice these skills are integrated into all curriculum areas, as well as schoolwide activities and celebrations that build a sense of community and belonging. Many of the interventions at this tier rely on children's ability to access areas of higher cortical functioning and language. For example, at the beginning of an activity teachers may ask students to set a personal goal that they hope to achieve by the end of the instructional block. The lesson ends by students assessing their progress toward their goals.

Expectations are adjusted to accommodate individual differences. For example, students who are unable to function in highly verbal, cooperative groups practice required skills in a smaller group of one or two students and an adult coach.

Children's capacity to function successfully with Tier 1 support is closely monitored. They are referred for supplemental Tier 2 interventions when universal screening or teacher observations indicate that they are not making adequate progress with only Tier 1 support.

Tier 2 Interventions. In a trauma-sensitive school, Tier 2 interventions are designed to reduce children's level of arousal to pre-trauma levels of cognitive processing, executive functioning, behavior, and performance. Emphasis is placed on interventions that soothe the limbic or emotional area of the brain, while restoring children's ability to participate in bonding relationships with adults. This capacity is often diminished by attachment failures in early childhood. Poor caregiving shifts the dynamics of the adult–child relationship from bonding to power-based competition. Interactions lack the safety one expects in early primary relationships. Children experience a sense of powerlessness within what should be a protective environment. These feelings trigger defensive reactions, including an increase in stress hormones and an automatic distrust of caregivers and teachers.

Tier 2 interventions usually occur in a small group setting facilitated by teams of teachers and mental health workers, who engage participants in ways that "surprise" children's mistrusting brains by violating their expectations of caregiving behaviors (Hughes & Baylin, 2012). Music and movement are integrated into group sessions that follow predictable routines and stress the self-soothing aspect of self-regulation. Some children find that deep breathing calms them down, especially when practiced in a playful manner with their teacher. An example is having children think of their fingers as birthday candles, inhaling deeply enough to "blow" all 10 out before they exhale. Other children find that yoga relaxes them in a manner that helps them focus on their work and become more efficient. Many chair yoga poses can be integrated into classroom activities with a minimum amount of disruption.

Interventions are designed to provide children with opportunities to explore the brain's interacting social systems, while at the same time learning how to collaborate safely with adults. Team leaders use a combination of playfulness, acceptance, curiosity, and empathy to (1) engage children in conversations about what it means to have a social brain, (2) teach skills children can use to understand others, (3) help children resolve conflict, and (4) aid children in developing strategies for enjoying and trusting the company of others (Hughes & Baylin, 2012). They may, for example, use role-playing to explore the emotions of others, or they may use trust-building exercises such as trust walks, where one child is blindfolded and has to trust the other to get them both safely to their destination.

Interventions at this level are reparative in nature. The goal is to stabilize or regulate children's arousal to the point where they can participate in social and academic activities relying only on Tier 1 supports.

Tier 3 Interventions. Tier 3 interventions are the most intense in terms of frequency and duration. Whereas Tier 2 interventions help stabilize children's ability to regulate their arousal, Tier 3 interventions help them achieve initial control of it. Children who require this level of intervention experience such overactivity in the brain stem area that their efforts to modulate impulsive or aggressive behaviors are continually thwarted. Interventions at this level are typically one to one. The goal is to re-create the circadian rhythm, or internal regulation of body states typically learned in infancy, through co-regulating experiences with caregivers. Interventions include short, repetitive, predictable, and patterned interactions; rhythmic movement; drumming; attempts at sustained eye contact; and joint attention. These are usually provided by an educational specialist with special training in sensory integration or cognitive behavioral therapy. In the case of sensory integration, services may be provided by an occupational therapist or music therapist. School psychologists or social workers are typically responsible for cognitive behavioral therapy.

The teacher's role in Tier 3 interventions is primarily collaborative. Teachers may be asked to accommodate the needs of children receiving this level of support by following recommendations of the intervention team and monitoring children's progress when appropriate supports are in place.

THE VALUE OF COLLABORATIVE PARTNERSHIPS WITH STUDENTS

Relationships with teachers offer children a protective buffer against the effects of trauma, especially when they are attuned to the underlying emotions behind their behavior. This buffering effect is even more powerful when teachers intentionally engage children in ways that promote personal agency and instill hope for the future.

Buffering Traumatic Stress Through Collaboration

Given the prevalence of early trauma among school-aged children, staff in trauma-sensitive schools anticipate the presence of at least one child with a trauma history in every classroom. This awareness allows teachers to take a proactive approach that engages children in collaborative partnerships. Characterized by respect and mutuality, these partnerships help minimize the effects of trauma and prevent additional re-traumatization. Teachers' nonjudgmental understanding of the nature of trauma and its persistent ability to derail interactions and learning helps them to anticipate unexpected outbursts and quickly restore children's sense of safety. Knowledge of the fragmented and sensory nature of traumatic memories motivates teachers to integrate sensory activities and self-soothing opportunities into instructional designs. They carefully construct conversations with children that help them rewrite their personal narrative of victimization and despair. They appreciate the timeless nature of trauma that can return its survivors to their original feelings of terror and hopelessness when triggered by events in real time. They know that will power alone cannot overcome trauma, but that caring relationships with teachers can. So they create classroom environments where the emotions behind children's overt behaviors are acknowledged and responded to. This provides children with the safety they need to cooperate with teachers, who can show them more appropriate ways to deal with unpleasant feelings. As a result, children are held to high standards but within the context of protective collaboration with supportive adults.

Preventing Reenactments

Children with early trauma histories or attachment failures are primed to mistrust adult authority figures. As a result, they often have extreme reactions to reasonable adult requests as these trigger traumatic arousal and discomfort. A mild criticism or perceived lack of a teacher's attention or understanding in real time sets off a reenactment of past terrors that children can neither understand nor explain (Farragher & Yanosy, 2005).

Knowing this, teachers in trauma-sensitive schools recognize these "bids for reenactment" when they occur. Rather than reacting to children's negative behavior, they respond in a manner that reflects their commitment to collaborate with children to overcome their past. When a child cannot break trauma's cycle alone, teachers step in to offer assistance. They quickly engage the child in a manner that interrupts the compulsive behavior and encourages a return to the current moment.

Fostering Personal Agency

Early traumatic experiences rob children of a sense of personal agency. This expresses itself in several different ways. Some children appear unmotivated, avoiding new experiences and quickly giving up when a task becomes too challenging. Others are unable to make a choice or state an opinion, seeking acceptance by following the crowd. Regardless of the presenting behavior, they expect to be victimized. Some continue to fight for control, whereas most simply withdraw.

Helping children rewrite their personal narrative occurs most successfully in classroom environments where teachers intentionally instill a "can do" attitude in children. They accomplish this by giving children a window into their own personal problem-solving process. For example, when an assembly is canceled or students are not grasping a concept being taught, teachers talk out loud about how they will actively resolve the problem or overcome the apparent obstacle. They reframe the canceled assembly as a perfect opportunity to read more of a favorite chapter book. Or they acknowledge that the instructional activities they are using are not achieving their goal and provide an alternative way of presenting the content.

By modeling an optimistic, assertive approach, teachers give children a new, more resilient perspective on managing the circumstances of their lives.

What Administrators Can Do

1. Provide teachers with professional development training on how the attachment process works.

2. Develop a schoolwide discipline plan that is informed by current research on the role emotional dysregulation plays in children's disruptive or hostile behaviors.

3. Model de-escalation techniques and restorative discipline practices in interactions with disruptive or hostile students.

4. Provide teachers with professional development training on how to work with the brain's plasticity to strengthen the prefrontal cortex and increase higher-order thinking.

5. Provide regularly scheduled time and coverage to allow tiered intervention teams to function effectively.

6. Provide leadership in helping staff reach consensus on the universal supports they agree to implement to support students at Tier 1.

7. Monitor implementation of agreed-upon Tier 1 interventions.

8. Demonstrate support for the tiered intervention team by frequent active participation in meetings.

9. Provide opportunities for teachers to meet with occupational therapists or school social workers who can assist them in managing the sensory aspects of trauma and in reducing the number of trauma triggers throughout the day.

10. Develop schoolwide policies on behavior management that reflect brain-based research on emotional regulation and relationship repair.

11. Provide teachers with professional development on behavior management techniques that focus on emotional regulation rather than contingency reinforcement alone.

12. Work with local agencies to create opportunities for students to contribute to the well-being of others in their community.

Frequent exposure to a variety of problem-solving strategies helps children persist at difficult or challenging tasks.

Opportunities to contribute to the well-being of others help children overcome the shame that characterizes their personal narratives. Since many children with early trauma histories have poor social skills, teachers find it best to shape their caregiving behaviors slowly, starting with the care of plants or classroom pets. With the right support and supervision, this

WHAT TEACHERS CAN DO

1. Use taxonomies of higher-order thinking skills (Anderson & Krathwohl, 2001) and neurodevelopment function (Levine, 2002) to select content area activities that promote prefrontal cortex development.

2. Use the data from frequent formative assessments to build children's awareness of themselves as learners.

3. Use flexible groups for activities that involve student collaboration to help children gain insight into the complexity of their behavior and that of their peers.

4. Use activities in collaborative groups in a manner that increases the speed with which children integrate new information into existing schemas by strengthening the connective fiber (corpus callosum) between the left and right hemispheres. Examples include interactive note taking and pairing new information with music or movement.

5. Confer with other members of the intervention team to develop Tier 2 or Tier 3 intervention plans for students requiring additional support.

6. Collaborate with tier intervention team members where appropriate to help children learn to stabilize (Tier 2) or achieve (Tier 3) psychological equilibrium or state regulation.

7. Collaborate with an occupational therapist to develop a "sensory diet" of activities that are appropriate for classroom use. Include simple movement activities like clapping or repositioning, as well as manipulatives that children can use throughout the day without disrupting instruction.

8. Avoid personalizing children's behavior. Instead, maintain an objective attitude with children that prevents reenactment of past traumas and provides the detachment needed to de-escalate behavior.

9. Create opportunities for children to change their personal narratives by modeling a "can do" attitude and helping them make meaningful contributions to their classroom community.

10. Provide children with opportunities to provide for the well-being of others.

approach gives teachers the opportunity to recognize children's contributions to others, while at the same time teaching them the skills they need for successful involvement with peers. When children experience themselves as valuable members of their classroom community, they acquire new insights about their capacity to make positive changes in their lives.

IMPLICATIONS FOR EDUCATIONAL REFORM

Addressing the needs of traumatized children requires providing teachers and school administrators with a new way of looking at children's behavior and motivation. Most teachers are trained to manage children's behavior through contingency reinforcements. Even those trained in applied behavior analysis base their interventions on the assumption that with enough reinforcement, children can learn to exert cognitive control over their behavior.

These interventions are seldom effective with children who have early trauma histories. There are several reasons for this. Lack of personal agency makes it difficult for these children to see themselves as the *cause* of another's behavior toward them. Erratic relationships with caregivers have taught them that rewards and punishments are more a function of the adult's mood than of their own behavior. Children find it difficult to impose a cortical "brake" on their impulses due to their characteristically dysregulated arousal.

Children with early trauma histories derive more benefit from a collaborative approach to behavior management. When teachers reframe negative behaviors as indicators of stress rather than defiance, children are able to use teacher-directed relaxation techniques to calm down and soothe the more primitive areas of the brain responsible for their reflexive fight, flight, or freeze response. With supportive coaching from teachers, children learn how to recognize differing levels of arousal and eventually employ self-soothing strategies to manage feelings of frustration or fear.

CONCLUSION

Integrating knowledge about children's neurodevelopment into classroom practice relies on teachers' consistent use of established best instructional practices. The relationship between differentiated instruction, dialogic teaching, and neurodevelopment is well established. The development of all children is enhanced when teachers create classroom environments that work with the brain's plasticity. With the additional support afforded by tiered interventions, these instructional strategies offer teachers an effective framework for buffering the effects of trauma while increasing children's capacity for self-efficacy.

CHAPTER 6

Nature's Second Chance

Constructing a Reflective Brain

The faculty of voluntarily bringing back a wandering mind . . . is the very root of judgment, character, and will. An education which would improve this faculty would be an education par excellence.

—*William James*

All teachers face the daunting task of eliciting the cooperation of a fairly large number of children for at least 6 hours every school day. This requires designing instruction that is robust enough to engage students with diverse interests and learning needs. Equally important is the teacher's ability to use careful observation, redirection, and contingency reinforcement or behavior modification to support children's efforts to behave in an acceptable manner.

This chapter provides teachers with strategies they can use to help children increase the reflective activity in their brains. Mindfulness training and other ways of improving children's awareness are discussed, as well as ideas about how to train children to use the analytical power of the left hemisphere to manage the emotional data stored in the right hemisphere. Collaborative discipline techniques, including restorative discipline, are explored. The chapter concludes with a discussion of resilience and its underlying neural signature.

SUPPORTING THE CONSTRUCTION OF REFLECTIVE BRAINS

The science of the last quarter century eliminates the need for theoretical discussions about how to promote prosocial, cooperative behavior in children. The data are in. The social nature of the developing brain makes it clear that the choices caregivers make about how they interact with children significantly affect the development of the neocortex. This is the area of the brain capable of overriding the reactivity of the lower brain that automatically triggers the fight, flight, or freeze response. Engaging children in a manner that fosters reflection, mindfulness, and systemic integration strengthens the neural pathways responsible for regulating feelings and behavior.

Fostering Self-Reflection

All children face the difficult job of learning how to inhibit impulsive behaviors, manage their angry feelings, and consider the effects of their behavior on others. Traditional classroom management techniques rely on contingency reinforcement to elicit cooperative, compliant behaviors. Trauma-sensitive schools use a more collaborative approach that teaches children how to use their minds to rein in their emotions and handle life's challenges or frustrations in a resilient and life-affirming manner. This type of emotional regulation begins by teaching children how to focus their attention on what is going on in their internal landscape. As they learn to watch their own mental activity, they discover two important aspects of attention: (1) that their internal world is full of sensations, images, feelings, and thoughts competing for attention, and (2) that they get to choose what they will focus on.

Daniel Siegel uses the analogy of a wheel of awareness to explain this phenomenon (Siegel, 2010). The mind or internalized self is at the wheel's hub. Sensations, images, feelings, and thoughts extend from the hub to the wheel rim. But none can command the attention of the hub without its permission. Attention always involves choice. And the best choices are those aligned with the goals children set for themselves. The mind gets to choose where it directs its attention based on the goals it sets for itself.

This is a very liberating idea to children with early trauma histories. They often have a compulsive need to focus on reoccurring memories of the past whenever they come up. These intrusive reminders of past traumas divert children's attention from events occurring in real time. Through the use of guided imagery, these children are taught to direct their attention to the sensations, images, feelings, and thoughts that foster happiness and enthusiasm versus those that deplete one's energy, triggering depression or lethargy. This ability to observe one's mental activity and make choices about what to pay attention to helps children release their past and imagine a better future.

Teachers help children take control of their attention when they conduct "brain scans" at the beginning of new units or lessons. This is a playful exercise that integrates another of Siegel's strategies into academic goal setting. This strategy is referred to as "SIFTing through the mind" (Siegel, 2012, pp. 226–227). It involves simply asking children to close their eyes and notice what they are *s*ensing in their bodies when a topic is discussed, observing the *i*mages that cross their minds, the *f*eelings that are stirred up, and the *t*houghts that take place in their minds.

Used in an academic setting, the teacher begins by stating that the class is about to begin a unit on the coral reef. Rather than using an activating activity that taps only into prior knowledge about the topic, the teacher encourages children to center themselves in the hub of their internal awareness. From there, the teacher asks them to review the spokes of their awareness wheel. Are there any sensations, images, feelings, or thoughts stored there that, if attended to, might help the student achieve the goal of learning more about the coral reef? Students are encouraged to write down any possibilities and select at least two that they want to focus on during the unit. One may decide to focus on the rhythmic sensation the reef makes as it sways in the water. Another may focus on the feelings generated in her by the fact that the reef is actually alive. In both cases, the attention is focused on points of entry into an exploration of the coral reef. Upon completion of the unit, children's awareness of the control they have over their attention can be further strengthened by a summary activity asking them to reflect on how making a choice about how to focus their attention helped them achieve their goal of learning more about the coral reef.

Teaching Mindfulness

The brain's plasticity offers hope to children with early trauma histories. Their early adverse experiences do not need to seal their fate. Rather, children can be taught how to use mindful awareness to strengthen the fibers of the middle prefrontal cortex, an area of the brain capable of modulating the terror triggered in the subcortical brain (Kaiser Greenland, 2010; Siegel, 2010). Mindfulness techniques teach children how to objectively observe their internal and external experiences—how they feel, what bodily sensations they are aware of, and what they are thinking about. As children simply observe their internal state without reacting to it, they learn to distinguish between who they are (the self) and what they are experiencing at any given time.

Learning to distinguish between one's self and one's feelings is an important step in helping children achieve emotional regulation. It allows them to observe their emotions before acting on them. This reduces impulsivity, as it helps children connect what is happening in their minds and bodies to their behavior. An additional benefit for children with early trauma histories is that mindfulness teaches them that they need not be helpless victims of their automatic thought processes. Rather, they can control how they respond to situations even when they cannot control the situation itself. This allows them to shift their negative conceptual framework to one that more accurately reflects what is happening to them in the present.

As children's capacity for emotional regulation increases, their executive functioning improves. They can control the focus of their attention and execute plans for achieving goals they set for themselves.

Mindfulness training is easily integrated into classroom conversations and community-building routines. Teachers do not have to worry about building blocks of meditation practice into already crowded daily schedules. Instead, they can use "mini check-ins" and "breath breaks" to encourage children to become more aware both of how they feel and how they can change those feelings by redirecting their attention to something more positive or soothing.

Encouraging Systemic Integration

Achievement of academic and social mastery requires children to be able to use various parts of the brain in a reciprocal, integrated manner. This poses a serious challenge to children with histories of early adversity. They need help learning to coordinate the functioning of four important neural structures: the left and right hemispheres, and the subcortical brain and the neocortex.

Research first published at the turn of the 21st century documents how early trauma interferes with the integration of the left and right hemispheres (Crittenden, 1998; Kagan, 2002; Teicher, Anderson, & Polcari, 2012). More recently, MRI imaging studies report differences between maltreated children and their typical peers in size and volume of the corpus callosum, the band of muscle that connects the hemispheres and transmits messages between them (McCrory, De Brito, & Viding, 2011).

The right hemisphere is very active in early childhood, absorbing bodily sensations, reactions to early interactions with caregivers, and strong emotions that can feel overwhelming at times. Caregivers who teach children words to describe or name their feelings help develop the left hemisphere's capacity to label right hemisphere data. Once the left hemisphere comes on line, children are able to sort, select, and sequence the experiences of their inner lives into a coherent narrative.

Children whose caregivers are unaware of language's regulating function often fail to link words and experiences. As a result, the right and left hemispheres are unable to work together to manage and explain the emotional flow of the right hemisphere. This integration failure is the cause of much of the emotional dysregulation and disruptive behavior observed in children with early trauma histories. When stressed, these children experience disintegration of their analytic, language-mediated left hemisphere. Their emotional, nonverbal right hemisphere takes over, causing them to react with uncontrollable terror and dismay.

The effects of trauma on the coordination of information passing between the subcortical brain and the neocortex are similar to that observed between the left and right hemispheres. Chronic exposure to fearful stimuli affects the development of the hippocampus, left cerebral cortex, and cerebellar vermis in ways that are detrimental to children's ability to integrate sensory input. As a result, the ability of the cortex to help children modulate the subcortical response to fear and danger is compromised (van der Kolk, 2003).

Within the school environment, these children are hypervigilant, always on the lookout for possible threats or rejection. They often display symptoms of compulsive repetition, or the need to engage authority figures in re-enactments of past traumatic exchanges with caregivers. Sustaining positive interactions with these children requires significant objectivity as well as the ability to resist personalizing their hostility and disrespect. Reframing these as symptoms of underlying terror helps, as does knowing how to de-escalate behavior by engaging children in collaborative dialogue about what is going on for them.

Children with early trauma histories need lots of opportunities to practice skills that strengthen the neural pathways linking their behavior and their prefrontal cortex. Frequent participation in activities that require higher-order thinking helps make the necessary connections. When appropriate, teachers provide the scaffolds needed for children to collaborate with others and solve difficult problems. Some children benefit from simple scaffolds such as scripted language they can use to greet peers or to make a bid to play a game or join an ongoing activity. Others need more elaborate scaffolds; a teacher could, for instance, facilitate conversation among a group of students, or rehearse with a child how to approach the principal about solving a problem before going to the school office. These opportunities strengthen the brain's executive functioning and thus increase children's chances of being able to override the reactivity of the subcortical brain in situations that require it.

USING TRAUMA-PROOF CLASSROOM MANAGEMENT TECHNIQUES

The goal of classroom management in trauma-sensitive schools is to pay attention to children's internal worlds while at the same time holding to age-appropriate standards for their behavior. Emphasis is placed on strengthening the connective fibers between the lower and the upper brain so that the higher parts of the brain can override primitive impulses.

Avoiding Further Traumatization

Another goal of classroom management in trauma-sensitive schools is to extend the amount of time children with early trauma histories are able to maintain a level of arousal that allows them to be receptive and capable of learning. Optimal arousal occurs most easily in an environment where adults are attuned to their needs and capable of establishing predictable and caring relationships with them.

As with all children, children with early trauma histories have a fluctuating capacity to behave appropriately based on their temperament, fatigue, developmental capacity, and situational demands (Siegel & Bryson, 2014). Some activities and relationships go better than others.

What is different about the fluctuating capacity of traumatized children is the intensity and duration of their reactions to trauma triggers. The terror evoked by these memories is felt in the deepest recesses of the primitive brain. Equilibrium can be restored only through access to behaviors that soothe the brain stem area of the brain (Perry, 2006). These include short, repetitive patterns of rhythmic, movement, or sensory activities. This type of sensory diet should be a part of a comprehensive classroom management system.

Restorative Discipline

Trauma-sensitive schools favor a restorative approach to discipline that is grounded in the relationships between children and the adults who collaborate with them in their development. Misbehaviors are addressed in a manner that strengthens these relationships, rather than alienating or coercing the wrong-doer. Restitution is focused less on punishment than on repairing the harm done to others by the offending behavior and resolving not to engage in it again.

Engaging children in restorative discipline practices involves training them to use the skills needed to address misbehavior and conflict resolution in an empathic and nonjudgmental manner. These include delivering affective statements, asking affective questions, and actively listening to what others have to say.

Class meetings or circle times provide a comfortable setting in which to model the collaboration and respect needed to practice restorative discipline. Role-playing with scripted dialogue can be used to teach children these new ways of communicating with one another. With enough practice, children come to see the effects of their behavior on the entire classroom community. When they make a positive contribution, everyone celebrates. When they misbehave or engage in destructive conflict, they learn that their actions affect everyone. But because they are a team, peers support the wrong-doer's efforts to make amends and quickly reintegrate him into the group for his benefit and that of the whole classroom community (Sprague, 2014).

The collaborative problem solving that is at the heart of restorative discipline is practiced within parameters that ensure children's emotional safety. Some classrooms use "respect agreements" (Claassen & Claassen, 2008, p. 41), whereas others use t-charts that list what respect looks and sounds like (Johnson & Johnson, 1985). Within this protective context, children become more aware of the thoughts and feelings of others. The ensuing dialogue increases their tolerance of differences. They acquire the cognitive flexibility needed to explore alternative explanations of events and situations in a nonjudgmental manner.

Classroom practices that foster restorative discipline include a desk configuration that encourages teamwork; a "peace" table, where children can meet to resolve differences; flexible grouping; and opportunities to work on projects that encourage perspective taking and negotiation. Some teachers find training in peer mediation helpful in implementing restorative discipline techniques, whereas others prefer classroom circles or short check-in and check-out circles at the beginning and end of each class. Whichever techniques are selected, the goal is always the same: to teach children that relationships can be repaired and old wounds healed when the goal is restoration rather than punishment.

FOSTERING RESILIENCE: THE CAPACITY TO SPRING BACK

Early studies of resilience implied that there is something remarkable or unique about children who survive early trauma and go on to live productive, meaningful lives (Goldstein & Brooks, 2014). In fact, there is nothing extraordinary about resilience. It develops within the context of children's first attachment relationships. The quality of care provided during this critical period lays down the neural pathways for the adaptive systems children need to manage stress. Problems occur when trauma or attachment failures interfere with the development of these systems. Interventions are then required to repair or strengthen children's adaptive capacities.

Schools are rich in their potential to help children restore a resilient mindset. Working with the brain's neuroplasticity, teachers are able to cultivate children's inner strengths, increase their sense of connection with others, and improve their ability to self-monitor their behavior.

Cultivating Children's Inner Strengths

The internal dialogue of children with early trauma histories often lacks the self-confidence and curiosity usually associated with resiliency. They typically have a poor opinion of themselves, fueled by attachment failures, abuse, or neglect. As a result, they tend to be pessimistic. Their characteristic "negativity bias" contributes to their apparent lack of perseverance or effortful control (Ayoub, O'Connor, Rappolt-Schlichtmann, Fischer, Rogosch, Toth, & Cicchetti, 2006).

Teachers can integrate several strategies into classroom routines to help children nurture a more positive attitude. One is to teach them the lyrics of songs that celebrate the benefits of positive thinking (such as "Happy Talk" (from the movie *South Pacific*), "Whistle a Happy Tune," and "You've Got to Have Heart"). Use these in impromptu sing-alongs when the class mood is spiraling down. Help children train their "resilience muscles" by having them respond frequently to four open-ended questions: "I have . . ." (state resources), "I am . . ." (state beliefs about self), "I can . . ." (state data-driven proof of performance), and "I like . . ." (state preferences) (Boniwell, 2012). This exercise increases self-awareness and is especially useful when teachers use the data-driven responses to the statement "I can . . . " to slowly change children's internal perceptions of their competency. Similarly, teachers' responses to the statement "I am . . ." is used to increase students' sense of purpose and personal agency.

Helping children increase their tolerance of uncomfortable sensations is another way teachers can cultivate their inner strength. The lower brain expresses itself through physical sensations such as numbness, tightness, fuzziness, or prickliness. Children with dysregulated arousal systems are particularly sensitive to these sensations, not realizing that they are of short duration, especially when one's attention is directed toward something else.

As children come to better understand how their mind and body work together, they increase their tolerance of intermittent discomfort, knowing it will not last forever. Instead, they can use "rebound skills" to feel better. These are tailored to meet individual preferences, and they include movement, visualizing an internal safe place, or withdrawing into the comfort of music or art.

Increasing Children's Sense of Connection to Others

Children with early trauma histories experience themselves as disconnected or separate from others. This sense of isolation has various sources. Some are the result of abuse or neglect. The burden of these family secrets causes some children to remain apart. Others lack the social skills needed to engage a peer, play a game, or carry on an age-appropriate conversation. Whatever the reasons, this combination of mindset and skill deficits threatens children's capacity to seek out the resources they need to move beyond early adversity.

Intervention requires a multifaceted approach that (1) re-establishes adults as safe, reliable resources, (2) teaches social skills, and (3) provides children with opportunities to get involved in causes beyond themselves.

Teachers as Reliable Sources of Support. Teachers who are attuned to children's emotional needs yet capable of holding them to appropriate standards of behavior restore children's faith in the ability of adults to help them regulate their feelings and behavior. Grounded in this foundational experience, they increase their capacity to view others as resources they can call upon for support.

Children become more comfortable asking for help and investigating possible resources when these behaviors are modeled by teachers. Classroom discussions about how to get members of the school community to contribute to class projects, and the assignment of peer helpers to answer questions and give support, are additional ways of encouraging children to access available resources.

Teaching Social Skills. Children with early trauma histories often need practice talking to peers and adults. Many have issues with language pragmatics that limit their ability to pick up on nonverbal cues or correctly interpret nuanced comments. They have difficulty forming questions and finding the right words to express what they are thinking or feeling.

Trauma-sensitive schools integrate instruction on these basic social skills into classroom circle or meeting times, as well as collaborative workgroups. When appropriate, children are given opportunities to preview vocabulary related to an upcoming conversation. Role-playing and scripted conversations also benefit children who lack experience in conversational discourse.

Service Learning. Service learning, or involvement in activities that benefit others, helps many children restore their adaptive capacity or resilience. Making a positive contribution to others teaches children they have something to offer. This is a powerful message when early experiences instilled the belief that they were worthless or nothing but trouble (Mullinar & Hunt, 1997).

Service opportunities include volunteering in the school recycling program, serving as peer models for younger children, or sorting materials in the art room. The only criterion is that these tasks be ones that need to be accomplished for the good of the larger community.

Some children respond well to an informal schedule of volunteer activities. Others need the structure and connection of a designated day or time to benefit from this intervention. In either case, as children learn to care for others, their capacity for self-care also increases. They become more confident in their ability to engage in meaningful pursuits.

Integrating the Experiencing and Observing Circuits of the Brain

The resilience of children with early trauma histories depends to a large extent on their ability to integrate the experiencing and observing circuits of the brain. Knowing that children in this population are quick to react to perceived threats, it is important that they develop the ability to objectively observe their feelings rather than simply reacting to them. Interventions that strengthen the neural circuits connecting the reptilian brain and neocortex increase their capacity to do this.

The simplest of these encourage children to approach the "big feelings" of their reptilian or "downstairs" brain with curiosity rather than fear (Siegel & Bryson, 2012, p. 37). Reassuring children about their safety in the present moment, remind them that there are many parts of their brain that they can get to know and integrate with one another When sensations arise that previously trigger fear, they need not face them alone. Instead, they can call upon the power of their neocortex or "upstairs brain" (Siegel & Bryson, 2012, p. 39) to evaluate the situation and determine if fear is an appropriate response. More often than not, feedback from this more logical part of the brain is able to restore calm and help children focus on what is expected of them in the present moment.

The integration of these neural circuits is critical to children's ability to move beyond the tyranny of the past by reducing the power of the reptilian brain to hijack their progress by triggering a return to the survival mode of fight, flight, or freeze. Their capacity for executive functioning expands as incidences of downshifting decrease, and different areas of the brain are better equipped to function in a more coordinated manner. As a result, children are able to engage in more purposeful behavior. They are no longer held captive by how their brains worked in the past. Instead, they have the freedom to allow new experiences to mold their brains in new ways. They are capable of moving on with their lives in resilient and life-affirming ways.

What Administrators Can Do

1. Provide teachers with professional development training on teaching mindful awareness in their classrooms.

2. Direct the attention of the entire student body toward improving the quality of life in some of the school community; examples include mentoring of younger students and fostering an attitude of belonging. Make a plan, monitor progress, change what's not working, and celebrate success.

3. Provide teachers with resources they can use to teach children about the brain and how it works.

4. Replace any fear-creating discipline techniques (such as time-out) with skill-building techniques (such as time-in, which is a mindfulness technique that can be used to encourage children to stop and notice what they are thinking about and/or feeling) that improves children's chances of managing frustration and disappointment in a resilient and life-affirming manner.

5. Develop a school climate that values diversity and seeks to increase reciprocal relationships between children and staff.

6. Hold monthly assemblies to commemorate school events and recognize students for their service and/or willingness to problem-solve.

7. Provide staff with professional development training that increases their understanding of the relationship between trauma triggers and behavior.

8. Develop restorative discipline policies that provide students with adult support to repair any harm they have caused to another student or to property.

9. Create a school climate where students are encouraged to participate in service learning in either the school or the local community.

10. Provide teachers with professional development on topics related to brain integration. Hold study groups using Daniel Siegel and Tina Payne Bryson's *The Whole-Brain Child: 12 Strategies to Nurture Your Child's Developing Mind* (2012).

11. Use data-driven proof of children's accomplishments to build their "resiliency muscles" and increase their sense of personal agency.

12. Foster a spirit of optimism in the larger school community by creating an attractive physical environment and drawing children's attention to things that are going well in the school at least once a day.

WHAT TEACHERS CAN DO

1. Support children's efforts at self-regulation by paying attention to their internal states while at the same time maintaining high standards for their behavior.

2. Use "mini check-ins" and "breath breaks" for deep breathing to help children remain mindful of how they are feeling and what they need to stay on task.

3. Use strategies that foster communication across the left and right hemispheres of the brain.

4. Intentionally engage children in collaborative goal setting, progress monitoring, and problem solving to strengthen the relationship between their behavior and their prefrontal cortex in a manner that improves their executive functioning.

5. Increase children's capacity to tolerate unpleasant sensations by providing them with strategies for redirecting their attention and feeling better.

6. Let children know that you are attuned to their needs but also capable of holding them to appropriate standards of behavior.

7. Teach children about the various parts of the brain, particularly those related to self-regulation. Show them how various parts can be taught to work together.

8. Teach children that self-soothing is an important part of self-regulation. Have frequent conversations with them about what they can do to feel better.

9. Avoid judging children's behavior. Instead try to uncover the emotion behind it. Introduce more effective ways of getting their needs met.

10. Provide children with easy access to a sensory diet that includes nonverbal strategies for calming down, such as moving, stretching, and deep breathing.

11. Use polling and other game-like queries to build children's self-awareness.

12. Hold monthly celebrations of data-driven proof of children's accomplishments.

IMPLICATIONS FOR EDUCATIONAL REFORM

Trauma-sensitive schools extend the resources available for effective classroom management to include strategies teachers can use to strengthen the reflective areas of the brain, thereby decreasing the impulsivity and poor judgment so frequently observed among children with early trauma histories. These include opportunities to set collaborative goals with children, as well as help them evaluate how effectively they were able to achieve them. Some teachers use the "TNT" strategy: when things do not go quite as well as planned, they ask, "What will you do The Next Time?" Others take time at the end of each lesson to summarize the content presented. Children are then asked to give a one-sentence "take-away idea." These are incorporated into the introductory activity for the next lesson.

Teachers avoid the use of threats or coercion, which reinforce the fear response of the lower brain. Instead, they opt for collaborative methods that help children activate their prefrontal cortex. These create a functional linkage between the child's experience of dysregulation and the part of the brain capable of returning them to a more comfortable, regulated state. Repeated experiences of this type strengthen the connective fibers between the upper and the lower brain. This improved communication helps children override the impulsivity of the lower brain and achieve greater control over their behavior.

CONCLUSION

Instruction that works with the brain's plasticity to increase children's ability to reflect and pay attention is the hallmark of trauma-sensitive schools. Classroom supports that are responsive to children's fluctuating capacity to manage their behavior strengthen the connective fibers between the upper and the lower brain. Students are able to integrate various neural systems in a manner that allows them to build their capacity for executive functioning and purposeful behavior. They become active participants in restorative practices that create a sense of classroom community while ensuring each one's emotional safety. Within this protective environment, children learn how to observe their thoughts, feelings, and behavior. Armed with increased cognitive flexibility, they are able to build up their "resilience muscles" and move beyond past traumas to create futures full of hope.

CHAPTER 7

Recognizing the Emotional Work of Teachers

We don't see things as they are. We see things as we are.

—Anaïs Nin

As the widespread prevalence of trauma histories among school-aged children becomes more apparent, attention is being directed at how prolonged involvement with these children affects the professional and personal lives of teachers (Perry, 2014). This chapter reviews what is known about compassion fatigue or secondary trauma among professionals working with traumatized children. Symptoms of this disorder are described as well as protective measures that teachers can take to avoid it. The possible link between compassion fatigue and teacher attrition is discussed, given the high rate of turnover that occurs among other professionals working with traumatized children (Balfour & Neff, 1993).

SOURCES OF TEACHER STRESS

Teaching is ranked as one of the top jobs associated with stress-related health problems (Johnson, Cooper, Cartwright, Donald, Taylor, & Millet, 2005). This is understandable when one considers the extraordinary amount of emotional work it requires. It is unique among other human service positions in "its emphasis on establishing long-term meaningful connections with clients of the workplace (students) at a depth not found in other professions" (Klassen, Perry, & Frenzel, 2012, p. 15). Every day teachers listen to repetitive stories of childhood fear and adversity in an environment where there is not sufficient time for recovery (Perry, 2014). In addition, teachers work within a limited range of emotions deemed "appropriate for school," even in the face of distressing interactions with students (Hargreaves, 2000; Zapf, 2002). They cannot, for example, overreact when treated disrespectfully or cry when overwhelmed by the adversity in children's lives.

Student discipline and motivational problems are frequently reported as sources of teacher stress and attrition (Gibbs & Miller, 2014; Klusmann, Kunter, Trautwein, Ludtke, & Baumert, 2008). This is especially true in situations when the behaviors interfere with the delivery of instruction to others (Chang, 2009).

Since these are areas of school behavior that are highly correlated with histories of early trauma and adversity, it is likely that teacher stress is exacerbated by the fact that the conduct cannot be brought under control by traditional interventions such as consequences, punishment, or contingency reinforcement.

In the absence of trauma-specific training, teachers fail to recognize trauma's symptoms and lack the resources to reverse its course. When teachers come to believe that there is nothing they can do to effect changes in children's behaviors, they give up trying (Jablow, 2014).

Effects of Teacher Turnover on Schools

Not only does the high rate of teacher attrition cost public schools in the United States more than $7 billion per year (National Commission on Teaching and America's Future, 2007), it also has negative consequences for many aspects of the organizational structure of schools (Guin, 2004). These include class size, curriculum planning, scheduling, and staff collegiality. These affect schoolwide operations and may indirectly affect the quality of instruction.

High turnover affects all aspects of school climate and is detrimental to student success, especially in low-performing schools with above-average minority enrollments (Ronfeldt, Loeb, & Wyckoff, 2013). It destabilizes the learning environment and disrupts the continuity needed to build trusting relationships among teachers, students, and families. High teacher attrition negatively impacts student achievement by reducing access to experienced teachers and the loss of the human capital needed for teachers to work together to improve instruction (Simon & Johnson, 2015).

Viewing Teacher Stress and Attrition Through a Trauma-Sensitive Lens

Just as traditional behavior management techniques fail to address the complexities underlying the behaviors of children exposed to trauma, conventional explanations of teacher stress do not capture the depth of distress experienced by teachers working with this population. It is not unusual for these teachers to report experiencing painful emotions, intrusive images, and an overall sense of helplessness, not unlike that experienced by the children they teach (Hill, 2011). In fact, any educator who works directly with traumatized children and adolescents is vulnerable to these symptoms of compassion fatigue or secondary trauma (Abraham-Cook, 2012).

Compassion fatigue or secondary trauma is characterized by feelings of incompetence and emotional exhaustion. Teachers experiencing it have difficulty maintaining the level of emotional detachment needed to manage one's feelings toward children whose behavior is frequently out of control.

Burnout develops over time, and its origins are almost always related to organizational factors like overloaded work schedules or a mismatch between skills and performance expectations. Compassion fatigue occurs when professionals feel there is nothing they can do to help the children they are responsible for no matter how much effort they expend. These feelings trigger a sense of hopelessness and can throw into question a teacher's beliefs about the meaning of life. Without intervention, teachers suffering from compassion fatigue often increase their involvement in escape activities, chronic overeating, and drug or alcohol use (Portnoy, 2011).

To date, very few studies are available that examine whether teachers' work with traumatized children puts them at risk for the mental health issues observed among others in the helping professions. What is known, however, is that in comparison to other trauma professionals, teachers get little training in recognizing symptoms of primary trauma in their students and virtually no training in the self-care needed to prevent secondary traumatic stress. This has serious implications for their effectiveness and rates of attrition.

THE BUFFERING EFFECTS OF TRAINING

Increasing teachers' understanding of the nature of trauma and its effects on children is an important resource in helping them manage their reactions to the experiences of the children they are responsible for. This awareness increases teachers' capacity to adequately respond to the social and academic needs of traumatized children, while safeguarding their own mental health and emotional functioning. Their risk of showing symptoms of compassion fatigue or secondary trauma is greatly reduced.

The Protective Nature of Trauma-Specific Training and Preparation

Trauma-specific training is a key component of building the capacity of teachers to work with traumatized children. Once they understand the biology of trauma and its effects on brain chemistry and child development, it becomes easier to master classroom strategies that are both self-protective and empathetic.

Implementation of a trauma-sensitive approach requires schools to carefully examine the assumptions staff make about children's misbehavior. Trauma theory views challenging behaviors as symptomatic of injuries children sustain in less-than-adequate relationships with caregivers. These behaviors are seen as less volitional or purposeful than many educators are taught to believe. This paradigm shift is a critical first step in helping teachers forge the collaborative relationships with children needed to overcome past adversity. Viewing challenging behaviors through a trauma-sensitive lens leads to interventions directed at restoring safety or a more tolerable level of arousal, rather than trying to manage the behavior with more traditional methods.

Changes in educators' perception of children's difficult behavior occur most successfully when training sessions are supported by ongoing technical assistance. Training content includes a thorough review of trauma theory and brain development, as well as information about compassion fatigue and secondary traumatic stress. Team-building exercises help staff reach consensus about schoolwide rules and expectations. This process stresses the importance of a consistent approach, while underscoring the need for buy-in by all staff.

Technical assistance activities support teachers' efforts to integrate what they are learning into classroom practice. These include small group discussions, book clubs, observations, and 1:1 coaching sessions.

Not all training topics require this level of support. Training on how to enhance best practices to accommodate the needs of traumatized children can be integrated into other curriculum training sessions and applied at team-level planning meetings.

The Benefit of Understanding the Teacher's Role

As mentioned in the introduction, the initial failure of trauma research to address the educational needs of children with early trauma histories limited the role teachers were asked to play in facilitating their recovery. The growing recognition of trauma's effect on learning, as well as the brain's capacity to restore itself with the proper interventions, justifies their greater involvement. The potential impact well-trained teachers can have on mitigating trauma's long-term effects is increasingly more apparent. Initiatives such as the Healthy Environments and Response to Trauma in Schools (HEARTS) program in California (Dorado, 2008), the Teaching and Learning Policy

Initiative (TLPI) in Massachusetts (Cole, O'Brien, Gadd, Ristuccia, Wallace, & Gregory, 2005), and the Compassionate Schools movement in Washington State (Wolpow, Johnson, Hertel, & Kincaid, 2009) are among the leaders in providing evidence for the effectiveness of trauma-sensitive instruction in changing children's lives. Unlike clinicians who see children once or twice a week, teachers have the advantage of spending several hours a day with them. When that time is used to create relationships that are safe, intentional, and optimistic, the results can be transformational.

Safe. Knowing that fear dominates both the external and internal worlds of traumatized children, teachers are on the lookout for signs that children are "downshifting" into survival mode or "upshifting" into reactive, aggressive behaviors. They are quick to offer reassurance or to direct children to self-soothing behaviors that help them return to a more tolerable level of arousal.

Agreed-upon schoolwide rules and codes of conduct are adhered to by all staff members. This consistency protects children from the stress and confusion associated with mixed messages and conflicting expectations of behavior.

Predictability is built into all aspects of the school day, including the schedule, the seating arrangements, and transitions from one activity or environment to another. When new or unusual events occur, children have time to prepare for them, and sufficient teacher support to calm any anxiety they might engender. Teachers use rituals to introduce and conclude instructional blocks. These rituals help children create the anticipatory set needed to feel secure in their ability to do what is expected of them.

Intentional. Teachers in trauma-sensitive schools have an intentional mindset that informs all aspects of the classroom environment: the emotional tone, the choice of materials, and the sequence of activities throughout the day. They are teachers who can readily explain why they are doing what they are doing.

Their interactions with children are particularly purposeful. They are directed and designed to connote the teacher's willingness to help children achieve three goals: (1) to manage intense emotions safely, (2) to learn how to use reasoning and judgment in the face of emotional arousal, and (3) to imagine a future where they control what happens to them.

Classroom discourse is characterized by frequent opportunities for "serve and return" interactions that restore children's trust in the ability of caring adults to notice and respond to them. Invitations to make predictions, hypothesize about data, and problem-solve as a team intentionally promote children's sense of personal agency and control.

Intentional teachers use ongoing formative assessments to monitor progress and student engagement, as well as to elicit feedback about children's interests and concerns. Data from these assessments are used to adjust expectations, revise strategies, and incorporate children's feedback into instructional designs.

Optimistic. As mentioned earlier, children with early trauma histories are stuck in the past. Their compulsive need to re-enact earlier experiences robs them of their ability to project a future where they can control what happens to them. Teachers cannot rescue children from their traumatic pasts, but they can help them move beyond them. When teachers encourage children to turn their attention toward positive experiences happening in real time, they increase their capacity for optimism. With repeated practice, children are able to "rewire" their brains in a manner that interrupts their persistent tendency toward negative thinking. Instead, they begin to scan their environment for positive experiences and increase their tolerance of positive emotions.

This cognitive shift has the potential to inhibit the automatic arousal triggered by negative emotions, thus enabling greater activity in the prefrontal cortex (Tugade, Frederickson, & Barrett, 2004). Expanding the lens through which children view their experience results in improved executive functioning and academic engagement. Children are better able to infuse ordinary events with positive meaning and to practice problem-focused coping skills rather than re-enacting past traumas.

Teachers use many strategies to help children develop an optimistic outlook. These include using class meetings as a time to thank one another for random acts of kindness, or having a "gratitude wall" where children record things they are grateful for. Some send thank-you notes to workers around the school, whereas others encourage children to share their gratitude for achieving certain goals or overcoming personal challenges. The point is to foster an optimistic, grateful spirit that resists the pull of recursive negativity, while offering children hope for the future.

Addressing the Contagious Effects of Trauma

It is important for teachers to understand how trauma affects those who work with its victims. Otherwise, they are at considerable risk of developing burnout, secondary traumatic stress, or compassion fatigue. Left unchecked, these reactions impact one's ability to provide effective instruction. Instead, teachers' behaviors begin to mirror those of the children. Feelings of fragmentation and isolation interfere with their ability to think and process information. A sense of heightened arousal makes them particularly sensitive to danger so that even minor threats trigger strong emotional, physical, and cognitive responses. Emotionally exhausted, teachers resort to reactive or punitive responses to student behavior that eventually create a "self-sustaining cycle of classroom disruption" (Jennings & Greenberg, 2009, p. 492).

Cultivating Awareness and Resilience in Education for Teachers (CARE; Jennings, Snowberg, Coccia, & Greenberg, 2011) and Stress Management and Resilience Training (SMART; Cullen, 2007) are two evidence-based models for developing teachers' social-emotional competency. Both emphasize the benefits teachers derive from practicing mindful awareness. Often referred to as mindfulness, this approach involves careful regulation of practitioners' attention, self-awareness, and self-compassion. This self-monitoring enables teachers to notice their own emotional triggers and avoid reactive responses to them (Abenavoli, Jennings, Greenberg, Harris, & Katz, 2013). Instead, they are able to maintain the objectivity needed to respond in an effective, intentional manner (Roeser, Skinner, Beers, & Jennings, 2012). In this way, mindful awareness helps teachers manage their own emotions and understand how their emotional responses impact others.

In addition to mindfulness training, both programs provide training in competency areas associated with reduced emotional reactivity and improved well-being in teachers. These include knowing how to set firm but respectful boundaries; demonstrating kind, helpful behaviors toward others; and managing conflict.

PROMOTING TEACHER RESILIENCE

Resilience enables teachers to persist in the face of challenges. Although some personalities appear more naturally inclined toward a resilient attitude, it is a capacity for adaptation that anyone can develop. Trauma-sensitive schools support teacher resilience by increasing access to known protections against stress, minimizing known risk factors, and preparing them to use their relationships with children in positive, life-affirming ways.

Components of Teacher Resilience

Teacher resilience is perhaps best understood as a dynamic process or outcome that is the result of interactions between the teachers and their environment. Three dimensions of teacher resilience are particularly effective in addressing the threats posed to teachers working with traumatized children. Good coping skills help teachers maintain the professional objectivity needed to help children gain control of their emotions and behavior without overidentifying with them or personalizing their rejecting behaviors. Self-regulation of attention and self-awareness help teachers manage their own emotions and notice how their emotional responses impact others. Finding ways to make a difference in children's lives restores teachers' sense of self-efficacy. Together, these three resilient practices sustain the sense of well-being teachers need to remain engaged and successful as educators.

Coping Strategies. Knowing how to cope with everyday challenges is a hallmark of teacher resilience (Parker & Martin, 2009). This involves having good problem-solving skills or the ability to seek out and use social supports. It also requires a level of impartiality that allows teachers to transform even the most difficult situations into learning experiences. Teachers employ this coping mechanism whenever their instructional goals are met with student resistance. The capacity to remain objective in these situations allows teachers the flexibility needed to appraise the situation and make necessary changes (Skinner & Beers, in press). Rather than personalizing the experience, they see it as an opportunity to gain a more accurate perception of student needs. It poses no threat to them or to the children with whom they remain engaged.

Self-Regulation. Self-regulation involves the ability to simultaneously monitor one's internal state while observing what is going on in the environment that is affecting it. The more aware teachers become of their physical reactions to stressful situations or emotionally charged interactions, the better able they are to interpret and account for them. This increases their ability to respond thoughtfully.

Self-regulation benefits all aspects of teaching but is indispensable when de-escalating children's behavior. It provides the internal support needed to refrain from reacting to overtly hostile or menacing conduct.

The better teachers are at regulating their emotions and behavior, the more equipped they are to anticipate the effect their words and actions may have on others. They carefully monitor their choice of words and tone of voice to ensure that they convey a sense of acceptance and connection. This enables them to bring a high degree of intentionality to their work, while avoiding the dangers of impulsive words and actions.

MAKING A DIFFERENCE IN CHILDREN'S LIVES

Children raised in healthy attachment relationships grow up expecting a certain level of give and take in their relationships. No one gets what they want all the time, but resilient relationships have sufficient elasticity to bounce back from misunderstandings. Secure attachment relationships give children the innate sense that "home is a place where, when you go there, they have to take you in" (Frost, 1969, p. 34).

Children with early trauma histories lack that sense of security. They overreact to perceived slights from peers, and indications of adult displeasure or judgment trigger deep feelings of shame. As a result, these children find it difficult to negotiate the social world of shifting and changing relationships. They are socially isolated from peers, who find them somewhat unlikable and prone to social problems (Jagadeesan, 2012).

Building Partnerships

Positive relationships with teachers provide children with the opportunity to acquire the security needed to form resilient relationships with others. This involves engaging children in partnership-building activities that help them acquire the self-confidence needed to participate in give-and-take relationships. As trust develops, children learn to manage their reactions to redirection and, finally, acquire the skills needed to use their minds to manage their emotions and behavior.

Redirecting Behavior

Being able to recognize and name what children are feeling is only part of what it takes to build and sustain trusting relationships with children. Teachers also need to know how to redirect their behavior in calm, respectful, and sometimes playful ways. This involves using strategies that communicate comfort and validate the teacher's connection to them. It includes reassuring children that the relationships they share with teachers are capable of containing strong emotions. This support increases children's ability to tolerate uncomfortable feelings and eventually become more capable of regulating them. Within this context, redirection becomes an opportunity to strengthen relationships and build children's inner strength.

Conversations that involve children's behavior feel safer when they occur privately, with the teacher at eye level and physically close by. Listening attentively to the child's side of the story, and using skillfully selected words

---

WHAT ADMINISTRATORS CAN DO

1. Provide encouraging, specific feedback to teachers that includes recognition of their contributions to the school community.

2. Provide strong, caring leadership that serves as a constant reminder of the vision of a trauma-sensitive school community.

3. Encourage teachers to regularly use interest surveys, conferencing, and other types of formative assessment to design student-driven instruction and reduce student resistance.

4. Use materials developed by the Mindsight Institute for Educators (www.mindsightinstitute.com) to increase teachers' ability to use mindsight.

5. Provide teachers with specific feedback on how individual children benefit from their emotional availability and support.

6. Provide teachers with opportunities to collaborate with mental health professionals concerning the management of recalcitrant student behaviors.

7. Schedule opportunities for experienced teachers to mentor those who are new to the school or the profession.

8. Provide the leadership needed to promote the inclusion of trauma-sensitive training into district plans for teacher retention.

9. Schedule trauma-specific training and technical assistance sessions. Arrange for classroom coverage.

10. Closely monitor the fidelity with which staff implement schoolwide rules and expectations. Hold reminder meetings when necessary.

11. Use songs, mottos, contests, and so forth to integrate an optimistic outlook into the school climate.

12. Provide teachers with opportunities to develop the social-emotional competencies needed to work in a trauma-sensitive manner.

---

to correct any distortions or misinformation, helps move the situation forward. The final step is to develop a plan to repair any harm the wrongdoing may have caused and to avoid future incidents.

Changing Children's Minds

Maintaining calm, loving connections with children strengthens the regulating mindsight circuitry in their brains (Siegel & Bryson, 2014). *Mindsight* is a type of focused attention that allows children to see the inner workings

WHAT TEACHERS CAN DO

1. Respond to student resistance with impartiality and a willingness to make the changes needed to increase or restore engagement.

2. Use self-awareness to monitor physical reactions to stressful situations and build the capacity for thoughtful reactions to students.

3. Engage children in partnership-building activities that help them acquire the self-confidence needed to participate in give-and-take relationships.

4. Keep an "efficacy journal." Get in the habit of taking 5–10 minutes to write down three examples of how your influence benefited one or more children in your classroom that day. Review the journal when you need a resilience boost.

5. Participate in online professional learning communities (PLC) addressing teacher stress and resilience.

6. Avoid personalizing children's behavior. Use meditation and deep breathing to maintain needed objectivity and emotional regulation.

7. Be on the lookout for increased use of escape behaviors to manage stress.

8. Commit to reframing recalcitrant behaviors as possible symptoms of trauma exposure.

9. Commit to viewing children's challenging behaviors through a trauma-sensitive lens that allows you to support them in an empathic manner.

10. Commit to implementing agreed-upon schoolwide rules and expectations.

11. Help children direct their attention to positive experiences happening in real time.

12. Use purposeful interactions with children to help them achieve emotional regulation and self-agency.

of their minds. Teachers foster this type of self-reflection by pausing several times during the day to give children a chance to check in on their thoughts and feelings. These "mini brain breaks" help children learn to monitor their state of mind. Mastering this practice enables them to break the cycle of traumatic reenactment by getting rid of ingrained behaviors and habitual responses. They learn to use their minds to take charge of their emotions and behavior. These mental and emotional changes are transformational at the physical level of the brain. By focusing on the inner workings of their minds, children are stimulating the areas of the brain crucial to mental health and well-being.

IMPLICATIONS FOR EDUCATIONAL REFORM

While recruitment of highly qualified personnel is a hallmark of recent efforts at educational reform, there has been little discussion of the stress associated with classroom teaching. Although seldom acknowledged, teaching requires above-average social competency and emotional regulation (Jennings & Greenburg, 2009). Many teachers are in daily contact with large numbers of traumatized children, yet they have little or no access to the types of support taken for granted at mental health agencies.

Future efforts at educational reform should provide teachers with the training they need to adequately respond to the needs of traumatized children, while protecting their own emotional well-being. Access to regularly scheduled clinical supervision and stress management offers teachers the recognition and support they need to adequately address the challenges of their chosen profession.

CONCLUSION

The prevalence of trauma histories among school-aged children suggests that schools need to proactively prepare teachers to manage the stress others report experiencing when working with this population. Teachers' work with traumatized children puts them at risk for compassion fatigue or secondary traumatic stress. Training that helps teachers understand the contagious effects of trauma can offset some of its negative consequences. Learning to successfully engage traumatized children builds teachers' resilience by increasing their sense of self-efficacy. Acquiring coping strategies that increase social competence and self-regulation fosters the self-confidence teachers need for continued involvement with children living in difficult situations. Together these skills enable teachers to maintain the optimism and hope that characterize trauma-sensitive schools.

CHAPTER 8

Next Steps

Managing the Necessary Changes to School Policies and Practices

Become the change you want to see.

—*Mahatma Gandhi*

The vision of trauma-sensitive schools as described here and elsewhere (Cole et al., 2005; Wolpow et al., 2009) runs counter to much of the organized culture of schools as they exist today. The lack of transparency that surrounds the prevalence of trauma in the lives of young children and models of student–teacher relationships that are coercive and disempowering creates an intimidating school environment for children with trauma histories. As a result, the risk of traumatic reenactment is increased, as well as the potential for further traumatization within the service delivery system (Harris & Fallor, 2001).

This chapter describes some of the changes in school culture required by the adoption of a trauma-sensitive approach. Suggestions for needed administrative supports are provided, as well as strategies administrators can employ to encourage teacher buy-in. The chapter concludes with a section on action planning, both in terms of personal changes staff need to commit to, and ways of linking trauma-sensitive changes to overall school improvement goals.

CHANGING THE CULTURE OF SCHOOLS

A school's culture is reflected in its unspoken expectations and patterns of behavior that reflect a long tradition of shared meaning. Staff construct this "hidden curriculum" based on common stories and symbolic gestures that they create and sustain through social interaction. The result is always part accumulated wisdom ("how we do things around here") and part a set of largely unconscious assumptions, behaviors, and beliefs. Examples include assumptions about what motivates children's misbehavior, appropriate teacher responses to infractions, and beliefs about how children's life circumstances affect their academic and social mastery.

Aspects of school culture that need to be addressed and changed as schools transition to a trauma-sensitive model include the persistent denial of the role trauma plays in children's educational failure, models of student engagement that inadvertently trigger the patterns of damaging repetition that characterizes the original trauma, and service delivery to children with behavior problems.

Confronting Denial of Trauma's Role in Children's Educational Failure

A school's cultural norms reflect the values and beliefs administrators and teachers hold about all aspects of the school environment. Traditionally these are based on intuitive theories or "folk pedagogies" about children and learning rather than on science (Bruner, 1996). Although they are implicit and out of the conscious awareness of teachers, these assumptions are powerful determinants of their behavior toward children.

A belief in children's innocent unawareness of the more vulgar aspects of existence makes it hard for teachers to accept the high prevalence of trauma and adversity in their students' lives. Similarly, the belief that children are willful and in need of correction makes the awareness that children's recalcitrant behavior is often due to injuries sustained by caregivers difficult to bear. Both beliefs and the behaviors that flow from them are potential barriers to a trauma-sensitive approach unless recognized and resolved.

As noted in Chapter 1, the prevalence of adversity and early trauma in children's lives is well documented. Until schools acknowledge the seriousness of this problem and commit to resolving it, the failure of other educational reform initiatives will continue. Trauma is not just a mental health problem. It is an educational problem, that left unaddressed, derails the academic achievement of thousands of children.

Service Delivery to Children with Behavior Problems

As our knowledge of the relationship between early trauma and children's neural development and self-regulation improves, it is clear that earlier efforts to help children with challenging behaviors often missed the mark. This is particularly true for children who are aggressive and difficult to control. When staff lack information about effective interventions for traumatized children, segregated placements in special education or alternative schools appear to be the only viable option. The labeling and stigma associated with these services only exacerbate children's internal experience of helplessness and despair. Separation from typical peers makes it impossible for them to learn appropriate behaviors (Kauffman & Badar, 2013), whereas the core issues driving their relentless dysregulation remain unresolved (Perry, 2006).

Trauma-sensitive schools resist the tendency of earlier models to segregate or exclude. Instead, they use formative assessment and tiered intervention to create a continuous feedback loop, linking student needs and teacher responsiveness. Staff are trained to notice "trauma flare-ups" and move in with additional support and comfort. Opportunities to practice self-reflection and self-monitoring occur throughout the day. Examples include modeling breathing control or another stress management technique at the beginning of an instructional block.

Self-monitoring can be built into the last 5 minutes of a lesson by asking students to discuss the connections they see to their prior knowledge of the subject matter, or by jotting down two or three ways they can use the content in their everyday life.

The Reenactment Triangle

Relationships in trauma-organized systems are characterized by what is referred to as the "reenactment triangle" (Bloom & Farragher, 2013, p. 91). Applied to schools, it illustrates the shifting roles children and teachers assume in the "rescuer-victim-persecutor" dynamic of reenactment. It is a largely unconscious process that is activated when children with early trauma histories either lash out against teachers in an effort to engage them as the persecutors in past traumatic experiences, or place them in the untenable position of rescuing them from a past that has already happened and obviously cannot be changed (Farragher & Yanosy, 2005).

Reenactment behaviors are triggered by teacher efforts at student engagement that inadvertently trigger traumatic memories. Physical proximity or using a loud voice activates sensory reactions associated with traumatic memories. Criticism or perceived disapproval produces feelings of shame, whereas an authoritarian attitude or unfair consequence sparks anger or rage. The intensity of these reactions surprises even the most seasoned educators. They may feel angry at the child for the outburst, or angry at themselves for not knowing how to contain it.

Staff in trauma-sensitive schools are trained to understand the power of the reenactment triangle to pull them into repetitive interactions with children that are "related to events that happened in the past rather than in the present" (Bloom & Farragher, 2013, p. 98). They know how to de-escalate children's behavior, as well as how to remain detached in the face of children's bids for reenactment of past traumas. Teachers recognize when students are getting stressed and are able to redirect them to self-soothing activities that are grounded in the present and capable of helping them move forward.

TARGETED AND NECESSARY ADMINISTRATIVE LEADERSHIP AND SUPPORT

Unlike other educational reform initiatives that require the replacement of the principal and 50% of the staff, the shift to trauma-sensitive schools does not involve this type of "turnaround" or "transformational" process. It does, however, require leadership capable of articulating and sustaining the vision of trauma-sensitive schools. Leadership should be inclusive, demonstrating a genuine interest in teachers' view and contributions. A robust collaborative partnership between administrators and staff members provides the support needed to overcome the resistance inherent in any systemic change.

Articulating and Sustaining the Vision

The successful evolution of trauma-sensitive schools demands that administrators understand the underlying paradigm shifts. Their ability to articulate a clear vision of a trauma-informed approach helps staff remain focused and see the changes fully implemented (Simon & Johnson, 2015).

The vision of trauma-sensitive schools is a web of collaborative relationships that ensures the safety of all within it. Trauma-sensitive schools are havens for children where the wounds of the past are healed and the challenges of the future prepared for. Adults are emotionally available and willing to support children's efforts to regulate their feelings and behavior. Personal narratives are rewritten as traumatic experiences are integrated into a broader context of caring relationships and positive experiences. Frequent opportunities for self-reflection help both staff and students maintain the flexibility and courage needed to cultivate the resilience necessary to move forward.

Administrators support this vision by creating the structures needed to implement the collaboration and emotional availability assumed by the model (Borman & Dowling, 2008). These include (1) scheduling common planning time, (2) creating partnerships with local mental health agencies,

(3) enabling teachers to get the coaching needed to manage children's trauma symptoms within the classroom (Spillane, Hallett, & Diamond, 2003; Warren, 2005), and (4) providing adequate coverage for teachers to actively participate in tiered intervention team meetings.

Practicing Inclusive Leadership

The collaborative nature of trauma-sensitive schools, as well as the radical changes they demand, requires administrators to create a professional school culture that encourages collegiality and peer support. Improving teachers' "social working conditions" in this manner provides an incentive for buy-in and sustained cooperation in achieving long-term goals.

Teachers expect administrators to take the lead in setting a direction for school changes (Johnson et al., 2013). They also expect to be engaged in the process of identifying problems, exploring options, and contributing to meaningful decisions.

Implementation of any school initiative depends on the degree to which teachers commit to embedding its principles into their classroom practice. This decision is based on teachers' perceptions of the administration's willingness to listen to their ideas and engage them as partners in the change process (Bryk, Sebring, Allensworth, Luppescu, & Easton, 2010; Johnson, Reinhorn, Charner-Laird, Kraft, Ng, & Papay, 2014). In the absence of a sense of shared ownership, change is gradual and most likely unsustainable.

Managing Resistance to Change

Change is always met with resistance. Even when it brings about improvement, it is difficult to give up familiar ways of doing things. But it is important to recognize that different levels of resistance exist. Early adapters embrace change quickly, often providing the impetus for others getting behind the new ideas. Others, though not at the forefront of the change process, enjoy taking risks and welcome the opportunity to get involved in something new. A third group waits to see what happens before committing one way or another. If the proposed changes are successful, they claim to have supported it "from the beginning." If the innovation is a failure, they are quick to say "I told you so." The fourth group is composed of "no way" people. They just do not change. Though approximately only 5% of any organization falls into this category, they can derail the change process if administrators spend too much time trying to win them over.

Effective changes occur in organizations where administrators reinforce and reward the efforts and support offered by the early adapters and risk takers. They can then attend to the needs of the "fence sitters" until the needed critical mass is achieved.

Making the changes required for schoolwide implementation of a trauma-sensitive school approach is more successful when administrators provide incentives to the groups supporting the initiative, thereby strengthening their commitment to the process. The knowledge that they have something to offer children with early trauma histories is a meaningful incentive for many teachers. Others appreciate the additional training opportunities that working at a trauma-sensitive school provides.

Teachers who are "on the fence" about trauma-sensitive schools often do not feel equipped to handle the behavioral needs of children with histories of early adversity. Some of their resistance comes from a perception of themselves as lacking the skills needed to make required changes. Others feel the new expectations expand the role of teacher beyond their comfort level.

Some administrators find that all these teachers need is the reassurance of knowing they will not be judged by the noisy or disruptive behaviors of children assigned to them. They need to be reminded of the collaborative spirit that characterizes the trauma-sensitive approach. Teachers and administrators work as a team. They rely on each other to lend a hand with children whose behavior is difficult and to offer new ideas to improve the situation. Other administrators find it helpful to give reluctant teachers an opportunity to visit schools that are already using a trauma-sensitive approach. Teachers who are still uneasy may need continued coaching and support to develop the confidence needed to fully embrace the initiative. Most teachers come to realize that, when provided in a collegial manner, embedding trauma-sensitive practices into their classrooms is something they are capable of doing. They realize that all children, not just those with early trauma histories, benefit from these practices.

CREATING AN ACTION PLAN FOR IMPLEMENTATION

The transition to a trauma-sensitive school requires broad, systemic changes. Administrators and teachers often wonder where to begin. It is a given that all schools need training and technical assistance to make the shift to trauma-sensitive schools. But individuals will most likely join the conversation at different entry points. Finding out what these are is an important first step in developing an action plan for sustainable change.

Personal Assessment

Achieving the goal of a trauma-sensitive school is best accomplished at the local level, where a strong commitment to inclusive leadership exists. The initial decision to introduce the required changes should, however, be made at the district level. Raising awareness of the need for trauma-sensitive schools usually takes the form of districtwide professional development. Initial training is often facilitated by outside consultants who are skilled at both providing an overview of the trauma-sensitive approach and persuading participants of its benefits to students. From there, principals and local school leadership teams can create action plans that are unique to their schools.

Action Planning Process

The action planning process starts with an assessment of what, if any, trauma-sensitive strategies are already in place at the school.

Figure 8.1 lists nine features of trauma-sensitive schools that are described here and elsewhere (Cole et al., 2005; Wolpow et al., 2009) to describe the approach. Its purpose is to identify the trauma-sensitive practices used by individual staff members, as well as to begin a discussion as to how best to generalize implementation schoolwide.

Once an initial assessment is completed, decisions are made regarding changes required to move toward full implementation. This involves (1) determining the order in which model components are addressed, (2) developing appropriate goals and benchmarks for each component, and (3) identifying additional required resources.

Changes of this magnitude do not happen quickly. Schools often decide to create 3- to 5-year implementation plans, with separate tasks and timelines for each component. This approach gives schools time to firmly establish changes in classroom practice that reflect a trauma-sensitive approach. These incremental shifts eventually become the norm and effect permanent changes in the school culture.

Linking Trauma-Sensitive Changes to School Improvement Goals

The changes required to implement a schoolwide trauma-sensitive approach directly affect what teachers do every day. Some of these changes involve the need to *release* values or patterns of behavior that teachers value or feel comfortable with. Teachers who rely on an authoritarian model of behavior management to bring out the best in their students may find it difficult to

Figure 8.1. Components of Trauma-Sensitive Schools

Component	Exists	Exists Somewhat	Needed
Schoolwide awareness of the need for implementation of a trauma-sensitive approach			
Regularly scheduled training and coaching provided to ensure staff understanding of how to implement a trauma-sensitive approach			
Policies and procedures in place that reflect an understanding of the need for strict confidentiality concerning issues of child custody			
Web of collaborative relationships in place to ensure safety and support			
System of tiered intervention in place			
Structures in place to support implementation (co-planning time, partnerships with local mental health agencies, coverage for tiered intervention meetings)			
Use of differentiated instructional designs capable of promoting children's neural development			
Use of classroom management techniques that combine recommended practices from the positive behavioral interventions and supports (PBIS) and social emotional learning (SEL) models			
Stress management practices integrated throughout the day			

release this belief to practice the more collaborative methods favored by the trauma-sensitive approach. Teachers who favor quiet classrooms may find the chatter and noise associated with student group work discomforting.

Similarly, the shift to a trauma-sensitive approach *expands* the teacher's role to include increased responsibility for children's emotional well-being and mental health. These changes require additional training and changes in their teaching style that some may feel is more than they "signed on for."

Teachers find these role changes easier to manage if they are linked to increases in children's achievement and their own job satisfaction. Integration of trauma-sensitive benchmarks into already-agreed-upon school improvement goals helps teachers remain committed to the change process. Celebrating small victories like improved class participation, less disruptive

What Administrators Can Do

1. Use the *Adverse Childhood Experiences (ACE)* questionnaire (see Appendix) to guide the record review of children referred for special services. If children have three or more ACEs, include a discussion of trauma's impact on learning in planning interventions.

2. Review the number of referrals to special education. Make sure that each referral includes documentation of the tiered interventions tried at each level and the effect of each intervention on student performance. If this information is not included, request to see it before moving forward with the referral.

3. Provide teachers with professional development on de-escalating student behavior. Participate in the training with them so that they know you are available to back them up.

4. Provide teachers whose behaviors may trigger trauma reactions with 1:1 coaching about how reenactment works and how they can use a more trauma-sensitive approach going forward.

5. Work with district-level administrators to develop a comprehensive professional development plan to raise awareness of the need for trauma-sensitive schools.

6. Work with district-level administrators to recruit and hire consultants capable of providing districtwide professional development on trauma awareness and trauma-sensitive schools.

7. Facilitate the process of integrating trauma-sensitive benchmarks into overall school improvement plans.

8. Work with teachers to develop and implement an evaluation plan that includes process monitoring and student outcome goals. Schedule times for both types of data to be collected and reviewed.

9. Display the vision statement of trauma-sensitive schools throughout the building. Use time at faculty meetings to highlight a section of the vision statement and brainstorm ideas about what that element looks and sounds like on a daily basis.

10. Monitor implementation of teachers' schedules to ensure that their time for co-planning and participation at tiered intervention meetings is not being lost to school emergencies or repeated interruptions.

11. Acknowledge teachers' contributions to the implementation of a trauma-sensitive approach by sending letters to central office administrators who oversee their performance.

12. Build staff confidence in their ability to implement trauma-sensitive approaches by giving them specific feedback about observations you have made about how well they handled a potentially challenging situation.

behavior, or fewer incidents of bullying is another way to encourage teachers to stay motivated. This is especially true when administrators connect these improvements with an increased use of trauma-sensitive practices.

Monitoring Progress

Evaluation is an important element of any action plan. It helps determine whether the action plan was implemented as intended and whether the anticipated outcomes were achieved. Although schools can use outside evaluators to monitor progress, other less costly alternatives are an option. One that lends itself well to evaluating progress toward a schoolwide trauma-sensitive approach is the formation of a transition-monitoring team. This team should consist of staff working in different positions at the school. Their purpose is to (1) monitor implementation of the action plan, (2) make recommendations for changes as appropriate due to changes in personnel or other unexpected circumstances, and (3) assess whether the outcomes are as expected.

In the case of trauma-sensitive schools, outcomes are measured indirectly through changes in student performance. Indicators are identified based on their known relationship to early trauma histories. With the exception of changes in social competence, most of the data can be mined from existing sources: school participation (improved attendance, reduction in times tardy), behavior (decrease in number of office referrals, suspensions, and referrals to special education or Tier 3 interventions), and achievement (improved standardized test scores and measures of classroom performance) (Cole, Eisner, Gregory, & Ristuccia, 2013).

Social competence is defined as the "broad set of skills necessary to get along with others and behave constructively in groups" (Child Trends, 2015). Although peer rating systems or nominations are often used to measure social competence, Child Trends recommends the use of a quarterly teacher survey that measures changes in children's ability to take another's perspective, work well with peers, resolve problems without becoming

What Teachers Can Do

1. Commit to increasing the use of evidence-based practices in designing instruction and analyzing student behavior.

2. Commit to learning how to recognize "trauma flare-ups."

3. Commit to integrating opportunities to practice self-reflection and self-monitoring into everyday activities and routines.

4. Help children identify self-soothing behaviors they can use in the classroom to relieve stress and feel better.

5. Come prepared to actively participate in co-planning tiered assistance team meetings.

6. Use part of co-planning time to develop strategies for embedding a trauma-sensitive approach into classroom activities and routines.

7. Provide feedback to administrators about how to best utilize mental health agency support.

8. Work with peers to create a school culture that normalizes the effects of working with traumatized children. This gives teachers the support they need to address those effects in their own lives and work (Rosenbloom, Pratt, & Pearlman, 1995).

9. Use the form "Components of Trauma-Sensitive Schools" (Figure 8.1) to identify any components of the model that are currently being implemented at your school.

10. Be an active participant in the action planning process in your school. Work with others to reach consensus on priorities and tasks/timelines.

11. Reflect on the role release or role expansion issues that will need to be addressed to successfully transition to a trauma-sensitive school.

12. Volunteer to be part of a transition-monitoring team or to work with colleagues to identify a measure of children's social competence to pilot at your school.

aggressive, and behave in a manner appropriate to the situation (Child Trends, 2015). Given the close association between social competence and academic success, this easily collected data can be invaluable in monitoring student progress as a function of increased trauma-sensitive practice.

IMPLICATIONS FOR EDUCATIONAL REFORM

Adopting a trauma-sensitive approach involves systemic changes that require close collaboration among all of the members of the school community. Unlike other reform measures that are implemented in a "top-down" manner, the paradigm shift required by a commitment to trauma-sensitive practices is so deep seated that it requires a team approach to be successful.

The philosophy of trauma-sensitive schools challenges significant tenets of some educational practices, while offering strong support for others. The challenges lie primarily in areas of behavior management and discipline where implementation moves beyond behaviorism to include a better understanding of children's emotional development. Strong support is given to instructional best practices such as differentiated instruction and dialogic teaching. These practices enable teachers to work with the brain's neuroplasticity to help children develop the resilience needed to overcome a traumatic past.

CONCLUSION

The goal of the trauma-sensitive movement is to firmly establish trauma sensitivity within school cultures and practices. Its success relies on the ability of administrators to articulate a clear vision of a trauma-sensitive school and to put structures in place that allow the necessary collaboration and support. The more teachers perceive themselves as partners in the required change process, the more likely they are to support its full implementation. Careful planning and progress monitoring help integrate trauma-sensitive principles into broader frameworks of school reform that are committed to improved academic and social mastery. Continued advocacy for the rights of disenfranchised children and recognition of the risks they face if their needs are left unattended or ignored emerge as fundamental issues to be addressed in any discussion of educational equity.

Resources for Professional Development

The following is a list of links to various training materials that provide information on trauma-sensitive schools and issues related to the topic. Brief descriptions of the training materials are included as well as the URLs where they can be found. The materials are available for anyone to use. The list is updated regularly. Go to www.acesconnection.com and click on Resource Center.

Strong Communities Raise Strong Kids (PPT): www.slideshare.net/JLFletcher/strong-communities-raise-strong-kids

> Arizona Regional Child Abuse Prevention Councils (2011) put this PowerPoint presentation together and has been showing it to dozens of communities across the state. It reviews the ACE study, brain research, the cost consequences of failing to prevent ACEs, and how families and communities can build resilience factors to prevent ACEs.

Childhood Adversity Narratives (PPT and PDF): www.cananarratives.org

> Physicians and ACEs experts from the University of North Carolina, Duke University, the University of California at San Francisco, and the New School in New York City developed a 50-slide PowerPoint presentation and PDF that the health-care community can use to educate policymakers and the public about ACEs. It might be a bit too complicated for the general public, but it is vlauable for people in health care who want to educate the health-care community.

The ACE Study & Unaddressed Childhood Trauma (PPT): www.theannainstitute.org/presentations.html

> Ann Jennings, PhD, of The Anna Institute in Rockland, ME, developed this overview of ACE study outcomes and health-care costs.

ACEs and Developmental Disabilities (PDF)

> Dr. Steve Marcal, senior director of Behavioral Health Services for the Center for Disability Services in Albany, New York, created this PDF to increase the awareness of childhood adversity among professionals working with developmentally

disabled children. The document can be used to train staff to be on the lookout for signs of trauma, and respond in an appropriate manner.

Adverse Childhood Experiences and Their Relationship to Adult Well-being and Disease): www.thenationalcouncil.org/wp-content/uploads/2012/11/Natl-Council-Webinar-8-2012.pdf

This presentation provides an overview of the relationship between adverse childhood experiences (ACEs) and detrimental health outcomes in adults. The presentation makes a strong case for medical professionals to include questions about childhood experiences when treating adult conditions such as addiction, obesity, heart disease, and COPD.

Children's Mental Health Problems and the Need for Social Inclusion: www.samhsa.gov/recovery/peer-support-social-inclusion www.slideserve.com/danton/children-s-mental-health-problems-and-the-need-for-social-inclusion

This PPT presents an overview of the issues that arise in helping children and families overcome the social isolation frequently experienced by children with mental illness. It is useful for agencies working with children and youth. It provides a comfortable framework for discussing the challenges involved and finding ways to overcome them.

The Effects of Domestic Violence on Children: Picking Up the Pieces (PDF): Nelson & Link. Legacy House. (2012).

Health Consequences of Violence and Abuse Across the Lifespan (PDF): www.ncdsv.org/images/FWV_ConBriefing-%20HealthConsequencesViolenceAbuseAcrossLifespan_4-18-2012.pdf

NCTSN's Assessment of Complex Trauma (PDF): www.nctsn.org/trauma-types/complex-trauma/assessment

The National Child Traumatic Stress Network (NCTSN) posted this summary in November 2013. The document provides an overview of the effects of childhood trauma on areas of child development such as cognition and learning. It is an excellent resource for teachers and school administrators.

NCTSN's Effects of Complex Trauma overview (PDF): www.nctsn.org/trauma-types/complex-trauma/effects-of-complex-trauma

The NCTSN posted this page in November 2013. It has brief descriptions of the effects of complex trauma on a wide range of areas, including attachment, body, brain, and economic impacts. Teachers and other professionals working with children will gain new insights into the behavior and motivation of traumatized children by reading this material.

Shift Your Perspective: A Trauma-Informed Understanding of Suicidality (PPT):
www.66.185.30.201/data/sites/16/media/webinar/tic-and-suicide.pdf

These excellent presentation slides were developed by ACEsConnection member Elizabeth Hudson.

Trauma-Informed Care (PPT): www.county.milwaukee.gov./ImageLibrary.../TIC-PPT.ppt

This presentation was developed by the Milwaukee County Behavioral Health Division. Administrators will benefits from this discussion of the change process required for full implementation of a trauma informed model.

US Military Studies on Adverse Childhood Experience (SlideServe): www.theannainstitute.org/ACE%20folder%20for%20website/53%20ACE%20questions%20in%20Military.pdf

An article examining the pros and cons of including the ACEs questionnaire in military health screenings. Results of the study indicate a resistance to including the questions unless confidentiality can be ensured. There were concerns that the information contained in responses to the ACE questions could have a negative effect on career advancement.

ACE Study DVD introduction (3 minutes): www.avahealth.org/aces_best_practices/appendix.html/title/ava-ace-study-dvd-and-online-videos

This video, produced by the Academy on Violence & Abuse, features presentations by and interviews with ACE study co-founders Dr. Vincent Felitti and Dr. Robert Anda, as well as Dr. David Williams, the Centers for Disease Control and Prevention (CDC) researcher who introduced them and participated in the study. Dr. Frank Putnam, director of pediatrics at the Cincinnati Children's Hospital, provides perspective on the impact of the study.

Childhood Trauma, Affect Regulation, and Borderline Personality Disorder
(1 hour): www.psychiatry.yale.edu/bpdconference/archives.aspx

A lecture delivered at Yale's Annual National Education Alliance-Borderline Personality Disorder Conference on May 10, 2013. Dr. van der Kolk discusses the relationship between early childhood trauma and the later development of symptoms of borderline personality.

The 3 Core Concepts (6 minutes)—Three short (2 minutes each)

Videos from Harvard University's Center for the Developing Child explain how toxic stress develops as a result of trauma, and explores how it affects the brain and nervous system.

How Stress Affects Our Telomeres (6 minutes)

The genetic structures called telomeres protect the ends of our chromosomes from fraying. As we age, our telomeres shorten. Stress (at any age) by way of stress hormones accelerates the shortening of telomeres. Neurobiologist Dr. Robert Sapolsky leads this segment from the 2008 documentary, *Stress: Portrait of a Killer.*

Dr. Gabor Maté: Importance of Attachment (14 minutes):
www.earlyadvantagebirth.com/2012/05/kids-culture-and-chaos-the-need-for-conscious-parenting-with-gabor-mate-md/

"We have to become conscious of attachments because the culture is forever undermining our attachments." Gordon Neufield and Gabor Maté, author of *Hold On to Your Kids* (Ballantine Books, 2006), is interviewed by Lisa Reagan at his Kids, Culture, and Chaos talk in Charlottesville, Virginia, in spring 2011.

Interpersonal Neurobiology (24 minutes): www.youtube.com/
watch?v-Nu7wEr8AnHw

In this 2009 TEDx Talk, Dr. Daniel Siegel explores beneath social and emotional intelligence and explores how they can be cultivated through reflective practices.

Violence prevention—Dr. Sandra Bloom (3 minutes): www.acesconnection.com/
clip/violence-prevention-dr-sandra-bloom-3-mins

In 2010, Dr. Sandra Bloom talked to the Congreso Internacional JUCONI in Mexico about preventing violence via community/family health. (The video is presented in English.)

Dr. Robert Macy—Communities & Trauma Informed Care (2 minutes): www.
acesconnection.com/clip/dr-robert-macy-communities-and-trauma-informed-care-2-min

It is important for professionals who encounter trauma victims—in education, business, health care, the courts, social agencies, government, and more—to understand how to recognize, diagnose, and treat people who have suffered intense psychological and physical trauma as children—incidents called adverse childhood experiences (ACEs). Dr. Robert Macy talks about why a community effort is important.

The Relationship of Adverse Childhood Experiences to Adult Health Status (93 minutes): www.theannainstitute.org/ACE%20STUDY/ACE-PUB.pdf

This is Dr. Felitti's original discussion of the effects of adverse childhood experiences on adult health status. It is a classic in the field that marks a turning point in the field's understanding of the relationship of childhood experiences to adult mental and physical well-being.

National ACEs Summit: www.instituteforsafefamilies.org/national-summit-presentations

The 2013 National Summit on the Adverse Childhood Experiences Study findings and their impact on health and well-being was sponsored by the Institute for Safe Families and the Robert Wood Johnson Foundation. Videos and PDF files of many of the Summit's presentations are available at the Institute for Safe Families website.

Adverse Childhood Experiences & Evidence-Based Home Visiting: www.nwcphp.org/documents/training/maternal-and-child-health/adverse-childhood-experiencess

This webinar (dated June 16, 2011) features Kathy Carson from the Office of Public Health, Seattle and King County and Laura Porter, WA State Family Policy Council from Washington State. According to the website, "New scientific discoveries about the lifelong impacts of adverse childhood experiences shed light on the intergenerational benefits of home visiting. Laura will share information about the ACE Study, including data from Washington State. Kathy will discuss some of the evidence of outcomes for home visiting and how understanding the impacts of childhood trauma can impact home visiting practice. This presentation is aimed at people working with young children and families and anyone interested in parenting and child development." PPT Presentation Slides.

Ask the Experts: Trauma and Stress or Related Disorders in the DSM-5 (42 minutes): www.istss.org/education-research/online-learning/recordings.aspx?pid=WEB0813

International Society of Traumatic Stress Studies experts present this webinar, which focuses on the implications of the Diagnostic and Statistical Manual of Mental Disorders, Fifth Edition (DSM-5) criteria for assessment within the context of treatment—with an emphasis on the changes as well as new items and criteria—and how they might affect treatment or assessment before or after treatment. Panelists also discuss the recognition of a dissociative subtype of posttraumatic stress disorder (PTSD) within the DSM-5.

Dr. Bruce Perry interview on Blog Talk Radio about parents who adopt children with early trauma histories (1 hour): www.blogtalkradio.com/creatingafamily/2014/05/14/parenting-abused-and-neglected-children

The purpose of this interview is to describe common behaviors observed among children with early trauma histories. Clarifies the difference between the threat driven behaviors of traumatized children. Offers parents strategies they can use to increase children's sense of safety and help them heal.

Creating a Trauma-Informed Team (Keynote: Ann Jennings, PhD; 93 minutes)

This webinar (2009) introduces the concepts of simple and complex trauma and discusses research related to retraumatization within institutional and community settings. The webinar is presented by the Division of Mental Health and Substance Abuse Services, Bureau of Prevention Treatment and Recovery.

The Impact of Trauma and Neglect on Young Children (1 hour): www.ctacny.com/the-impact-of-trauma-and-neglect-on-young-children.html

Dr. Bruce Perry presents this webinar from the New York Clinical Technical Assistance Center.

Reclaiming Futures: Communities Helping Teens Overcome Drugs, Alcohol, & Crime: www.reclaimingfutures.org/webinars

New webinars are hosted almost every month by invited experts, and archived webinars are available on such topics as juvenile justice reform, juvenile drug courts, adolescent substance abuse treatment, and positive youth development.

THRIVE's Trauma-Informed Webinar Trainings: www.thriveinitiative.org/trauma-informed/training/

THRIVE webinars embody System of Care principles and are well suited for agency orientations, and group or individual viewing. Registration for each webinar is required, and will give access to the Guide to Trauma-Informed Organizational Development and other resources. THRIVE is Maine's graduated System of Care, and receives funding from Maine's Department of Corrections Division of Juvenile Services and the federal Substance Abuse and Mental Health Services Administration.

Trauma: A Public Health Crisis in Western New York Conference: socialwork.buffalo.edu/social-research/institutes-centers/institute-on-trauma-and-trauma-informed-care/community-partnership-initiaties/community-partnerships.html

This webinar features Dr. Sandra Bloom and Dr. Robert Anda, who on March 12 and 13, 2010, spoke at the Trauma: A Public Health Crisis in Western New York conference, sponsored by the Community Health Foundation of Western and Central New York. Conference participants learned to recognize the role of trauma in the lives of children, to identify the effects of adverse childhood experiences on adult health risk behaviors and diseases, and to apply the tenets of the Sanctuary Model to provide trauma-informed treatment and care. Furthermore, this conference enabled participants to collaborate with one another to form a network of community leaders and activists.

Trauma-Informed Care for Women Experiencing Homelessness and Their Children (59 minutes): www.usich.gov/media-center/videos-and-webinars/tic-webinar

This webinar, sponsored by the US Interagency Council on Homelessness, explores the ways homeless services programs can use a trauma-informed care model to better serve mothers and their children and help break through the cycle of trauma and homelessness. The goal of the webinar (dated May 9, 2012) is to share information on how to improve the trauma confidence of your organization.

Trauma-Informed Practice with Children and Youth in the Child Welfare System (65 minutes): www.nrcpfc.org/webcasts/28.html

This webcast features Erika Tullberg—an assistant professor of research at the New York University Child Study Center and director of the Atlas Project, an Administration for Children and Families–funded effort to address trauma and other mental health issues in New York State's child welfare system—and Dr. Glenn N. Saxe (the Arnold Simon Professor and Chair, Department of Child and Adolescent Psychiatry, New York University Child Study Center), a physician -scientist with a focus on the psychiatric consequences of traumatic events in children. The focus of the webinar is foster care and birth parents. Other resources are included on this website. The webinar (dated February 6, 2013) is sponsored by the National Resource Center for Permanency and Family Connections.

Treating Trauma in Kids (1 hour): www.ewclaimingfutures.org/resources/webinars

Charles Wilson, executive director of the Chadwick Center for Children and Families at Rady Children's Hospital–San Diego, describes his work developing a trauma-informed systems approach that treats children within the child welfare system. This presentation (dated May 27, 2010) is applicable to the field of juvenile justice as well.

Finding Your ACE Score

While you were growing up, during your first 18 years of life:

1. Did a parent or other adult in the household often or very often swear at you, insult you, put you down, or humiliate you? Or act in a way that made you afraid that you might be physically hurt?
   Yes   No   If yes enter 1 _____
2. Did a parent or other adult in the household often or very often push, grab, slap, or throw something at you? Or ever hit you so hard that you had marks or were injured?
   Yes   No   If yes enter 1 _____
3. Did an adult or person at least 5 years older than you ever touch or fondle you or have you touch their body in a sexual way? Or attempt or actually have oral, anal, or vaginal intercourse with you?
   Yes   No   If yes enter 1 _____
4. Did you often or very often feel that no one in your family loved you or thought you were important or special? Or your family didn't look out for each other, feel close to each other, or support each other?
   Yes   No   If yes enter 1 _____
5. Did you often or very often feel that you didn't have enough to eat, had to wear dirty clothes, and had no one to protect you? Or your parents were too drunk or high to take care of you or take you to the doctor if you needed it?
   Yes   No   If yes enter 1 _____
6. Were your parents ever separated or divorced?
   Yes   No   If yes enter 1 _____
7. Was your mother or stepmother:
   Often or very often pushed, grabbed, slapped, or had something thrown at her?
   Or sometimes, often, or very often kicked, bitten, hit with a fist, or hit with something hard? Or ever repeatedly hit at least a few minutes or threatened with a gun or knife?
   Yes   No   If yes enter 1 _____

8. Did you live with anyone who was a problem drinker or alcoholic or who used street drugs?

  Yes   No   If yes enter 1 _____

9. Was a household member depressed or mentally ill, or did a household member attempt suicide?

  Yes   No   If yes enter 1 _____

10. Did a household member go to prison?

  Yes   No   If you yes enter 1 _____

Now add up your"YES" answers: This is your ACE score.

(Retrieved   from   www.acestudy.org/yahoo_site_admin/assets/docs/ACE_ Calculator-English.127193712.pdf)

References

ABA Juvenile Justice Committee, Zero Tolerance Policy Report. (2001). Washington, DC: Author.

Abenavoli, R. M., Jennings, P. A., Greenburg, M. T., Harris, A. R., & Katz, D. A. (2013). The protective effects of mindfulness against burnout among educators. *Psychology of Education Review, 37*(2), 57–69.

Abraham-Cook, S. (2012). *The prevalence and correlates of compassion fatigue, compassion satisfaction, and burnout among teachers working in high-poverty urban public schools* (Doctoral dissertation, Seton Hall University). Retrieved from http://scholarship.shu.edu/cgi/viewcontent.cgi?article=2820&context=dissertations

Anderson, L. W., & Krathwohl, D. R. (2001). *A taxonomy for learning, teaching, and assessing: A revision of Bloom's taxonomy of educational objectives.* New York, NY: Longman.

Annie E. Casey Foundation. (2013). *Early warning confirmed: A research update on third grade reading.* Baltimore, MD: Author. Retrieved from www.aecf.org/resources/early-warning-confirmed/

Asam, K. (2015). *Trauma-sensitive schools.* Burlington, VT: University of Vermont.

Ayoub, C. C., O'Connor, E., Rappolt-Schlichtmann, G., Fischer, K. W., Rogosch, F. A., Toth, S. L., & Cicchetti, D. (2006). Cognitive and emotional differences in young maltreated children: A translational application of dynamic skill theory. *Development and Psychopathology, 18,* 679–706. doi:10.1017S0954579406060342

Babcock, E. (2014). *Using brain research to design new pathways out of poverty.* Brighton, MA: Crittendon Women's Union.

Badger, E. (2013, August 29). How poverty taxes the brain. *The Atlantic City Lab.* Retrieved from http://www.citylab.com/work/2013/08/how-poverty-taxes-brain/6716/

Balfour, D., & Neff, P. (1993). Predicting and managing turnover in human service agencies: A case study of an organization in crisis. *Public Personnel Management, 22,* 473–486. doi:10.1177/009102609302200310

Belsky, J., & Haan, M. D. (2011). Annual research review: Parenting and children's brain development: The end of the beginning. *Journal of Child Psychology and Psychiatry, 52,* 409–428. doi:10.1111/j.1469-7610.2010.02281.x

Beltman, S., Mansfield, C., & Price, A. (2011). Thriving not just surviving: A review of research on teacher resilience. *Educational Research Review, 6,* 185–207. doi:10.1016/j.edurev.2011.09.001

Bergin, C., & Bergin, D. (2009). Attachment in the classroom. *Educational Psychology Review, 21,* 141–170. doi: 10.1007/s10648-009-9104-0

Blair, C., & Razza, R. P. (2007). Relating effortful control, executive function, and false belief understanding to emerging math and literacy ability in kindergarten. *Child Development, 78*, 647–663. doi:0.1111/j.1467-8624.2007.01019.x

Bloom, S. L., & Farragher, B. (2011). *Destroying sanctuary: The crisis in human service delivery systems.* New York, NY: Oxford University Press.

Bloom, S. L., & Farragher, B. (2013). *Restoring sanctuary: A new operating system for trauma-informed systems of care.* New York, NY: Oxford University Press.

Bogolepova, I. N., & Malofeeva, L. I. (2001). Characteristics of the development of speech motor areas 44 and 45 in the left and right hemisphere of the human brain in early post-natal ontogenesis. *Neuroscience and Behavioral Physiology, 31*, 349–354. doi:10.1023/A:1010468007795

Boniwell, I. (2012). *Positive psychology in a nutshell.* New York, NY: McGraw Hill.

Borman, G. D., & Dowling, N. M. (2008). Teacher attrition and retention: A meta-analytic and narrative review of the research. *Review of Educational Research, 78*, 367–409. doi:10.3102/0034654308321455

Brackett, M., & Rivers, S. (2014). Transforming students' lives with social and emotional learning. In Reinhart Pekrun & Lisa Linnerbrink-Garcia (Eds.) *International handbook of emotions in education* (pp. 368–388). New York, NY: Routledge.

Briere, J., & Spinazzola, J. (2005). Phenomenology and psychological assessment of complex posttraumatic stress. *Journal of Traumatic Stress, 18*, 401–412. doi:10.1002/jts.20048

Bruner, J. (1996). *The culture of education.* Cambridge, MA: Harvard University Press.

Bryk, A. S., Sebring, P. B., Allensworth, E., Luppescu, S., & Easton, J. Q. (2010). *Organizing schools for improvement: Lessons from Chicago.* Chicago, IL: University of Chicago Press.

Caine, R., & Caine, G. (1990). Understanding a brain-based approach to learning and teaching. *Educational Leadership,* 66–70.

Casey, B. J., Jones, R. M., & Somerville, L. H. (2011). Braking and accelerating of the adolescent brain. *Journal of Research on Adolescence, 21*, 21–33. doi:10.1111/j.1532-7795.2010.00712.x

CAST. (2011). *Universal Design for Learning Guidelines version 2.0.* Retrieved from http://www.udlcenter.org/aboutudl/udlguidelines

Center for Youth Wellness. (2014). *An unhealthy dose of stress* [White paper]. Retrieved from http://bit.ly/ACEswhitepaper

Chang, M. L. (2009). An appraisal perspective of teacher burnout: Examining the emotional work of teachers. *Educational Psychology Review, 21*, 193–218. doi:10.1007/s10648-009-9106-y

Child Trends (2015). *Social competence #14.* Retrieved from www.childtrends.org/our-research/positive-indicators/positive-indicators-project/social-competence

Claassen, R., & Claassen, R. (2008). *Discipline that restores: Strategies to create respect, cooperation, and responsibility in the classroom.* Charleston, SC: BookSurge Publishing.

Cloitre, M., Stolbach, B. C., Herman, J. L., van der Kolk, B., Pynoos, R., Wang, J., & Petkova, E. (2009). A developmental approach to complex PTSD: Childhood and adult cumulative trauma as predictors of system complexity. *Journal of Traumatic Stress, 22*, 399–408. doi:10.1002/jts.20444

Cole, S. F., O'Brien, J. G., Gadd, M. G., Ristuccia, J., Wallace, D. L., & Gregory, M. (2005). *Helping traumatized children learn: Supportive school environments for children traumatized by family violence.* Boston, MA: Massachusetts Advocates for Children and Harvard Law School, Trauma and Learning Policy Initiative. Retrieved from www.traumasensitiveschools.org

Cole, S., Eisner, A., Gregory, M., & Ristuccia, J. (2013). *Creating and advocating for trauma-sensitive schools.* Boston, MA: Massachusetts Advocates for Children and Harvard Law School, Trauma and Learning Policy Initiative. Retrieved from www.traumasensitiveschools.org

Collaborative for Academic, Social, and Emotional Learning. (2004). *Creating connections for student success: The CASEL 2003 annual report.* Retrieved from http://static1.squarespace.com/static/513f79f9e4b05ce7b70e9673/t/526a22f3e-40f35a9effc404/1382687475283/creating-connections-for-student-success.pdf

Cook, A., Blaustein, M., Spinazzola, J., & van der Kolk, B. (2003). *Complex trauma in children and adolescents* [White paper]. Retrieved from National Child Traumatic Stress Network website: http://www.nctsnet.org/nctsn_assets/pdfs/edu_materials/ComplexTrauma_All.pdf

Cook, A., Spinazzola, J., Ford, J., Lanktree, C., Blaustein, M., Sprague, C., . . . van der Kolk, B. (2007). Complex trauma in children and adolescents. *Focal Point, 21*(1), 4–8.

Cozolino, L. J. (2013). *The social neuroscience of education: Optimizing attachment and learning in the classroom.* New York, NY: Norton.

Craig, S. E. (1992). The educational needs of children living in violence. *Phi Delta Kappan, 74*(1), 67–71.

Craig, S. E. (2001, January 16). Remarks at Helping Traumatized Children Learn, a conference sponsored by Lesley College, Massachusetts Advocates for Children (MAC), and the Task Force on Children Affected by Domestic Violence, Cambridge, MA. (Transcripts of the conference are on file at Massachusetts Advocates for Children, 25 Kingston St, 2nd Floor, Boston, MA 02111)

Craig, S. E. (2008). *Reaching and teaching children who hurt: Strategies for your classroom.* Baltimore, MD: Brookes Publishing Co.

Crespi, B. J. (2011). The strategies of the genes: Genomic conflicts, attachment theory, and development of the social brain. In A. Petronis, & J. Mill (Eds.), *Brain, behavior, and epigenetics* (pp. 143–167). Heidelberg, Germany: Springer-Verlag.

Crittenden, P. M. (1998). Dangerous behaviors and dangerous contexts: A 35-year perspective on research on the developmental effects of child physical abuse. In P. K. Trickett, & C. J. Schellenbach (Eds.), *Violence against children in the family and the community* (pp. 11–38). Washington, DC: APA.

Cullen, M. (2007). Stress management and resilience training: Stopping teacher burn-out, Greater good: The science of a meaningful life.

Davis, G.M., & Logie, R.L. (Eds.) (1993). *Memory in everyday life.* Amsterdam: Elsevier.

Dianis, J. B. (2012, December 13). It's time for common sense school discipline. *Huffington Post.* Retrieved from www.huffingtonpost.com/judith-browne-dianis/its-time-for-common-sense_b_2285241.html

D'Andrea, W., Ford, J., Stolbach, B., Spinazzola, J., & van der Kolk, B. A. (2012). Understanding interpersonal trauma in children: Why we need a developmentally appropriate trauma diagnosis. *Journal of Orthopsychiatry, 82,* 187–200. doi:10.1111/j.1939-0025.2012.01154.x

De Bellis, M.D. & Kuchibhatla, M. (2006). Cerebellar volumes in pediatric mal-treatment related post-traumatic stress disorder. *Biological Psychiatry 60*, 697–703.

Dorado, J. (2008) *Healthy environments and response to trauma in schools*. San Francisco, CA: University of California, San Francisco.

Duncan, G., & Murnane, R. (2011). Economic inequality: Cause of urban school problems. *Chicago Tribune*. Retrieved from http://articles.chicagotribune.com/2011-10-06/opinion/ct-perspec-10061-urban-20111006_1_poor-children-graduation-rate-gap

Elais, M. (2013). The school-to-prison pipeline. *Teaching Tolerance, 43, 39–40*.

Ensor, P. (1988). The functional silo syndrome. AME Target (p. 16). Rolling Meadows, IL: Association for Manufacturing Excellence.

Farragher, B., & Yanosy, S. (2005). Creating a trauma-sensitive culture in residential treatment. *Therapeutic Communities: The International Journal for Therapeutic and Supportive Organizations, 26, 96–113*.

Felitti, V. J., Anda, R. F., Nordenberg, D., Williamson, D. F., Spitz, A. M., Edwards, V., & Marks, J. S. (1998). Relationship of childhood abuse and household dysfunction to many of the leading causes of death in adults: The adverse childhood experiences (ACE) study. *American Journal of Preventive Medicine, 14*, 245–258. doi:10.1016/S0749-3797(98)00017-8

Figley, C. R. (Ed.). (2002). *Treating compassion fatigue*. New York, NY: Brunner/Mazel.

Finkelhor, D., Ormod, R. K., & Turner, H. A. (2007). Poly-victimization: A neglected component in child victimization. *Child Abuse and Neglect, 31, 7–26*. doi:10.1016/j.chiabu.2006.06.008

Finkelhor, D., Turner, H. A., Ormod, R. K., & Hamby, S. L. (2010). Trends in childhood violence and abuse exposure: Evidence from two national surveys. *Archives of Pediatrics and Adolescent Medicine, 164, 238–242*.

Ford, J. D., & Russo, E. (2006). Trauma focused, present centered, emotional self-regulation approach to treatment for post-traumatic stress and addiction: Training adaptive recovery group education and therapy (TARGET). *American Journal of Psychotherapy, 60, 355–555*.

Frost, R. (1969). *The poetry of Robert Frost: The collected poems, complete and unabridged*. New York, NY: Henry Holt.

Garbarino, J., Dubrow, N., Kostelny, K., & Pardo, C. (1992). *Children in danger: Coping with the consequences of community violence*. San Francisco, CA: Jossey-Bass.

Gibbs, S., & Miller, A. (2014). Teachers' resilience and well-being: A role for educational psychology. *Teachers and Teaching: Theory and Practice, 20, 609–621*. doi:10.1080/13540602.2013.844408

Goldstein, S., & Brooks, R. B. (Eds.). (2014). *Handbook of resiliency in children*. New York, NY: Springer Media.

Green, E. (2014). *Building a better teacher: How teaching works (and how to teach it to everyone)*. New York, NY: Norton.

Gross, T. (2013). Hippocampus involvement in explicit memory processes related to trauma. *School Psychology: From Science to Practice, 6(3), 21–27*.

Groves, B. M. (2002). *Children who see too much*. Boston, MA: Beacon Press.

Guin, K. (2004). Chronic teacher turnover in urban elementary schools. *Educational*

Policy Analysis Archives, 12(42), 1–25. Retrieved from epaa.asu.edu/ojs/article/view/197

Haller, L., & LaPierre, A. (2012). *Healing developmental trauma: How early trauma affects self-regulation, self-image and the capacity for relationship.* Berkeley, CA: North Atlantic Books.

Hamby, S., Finkelhor, D., Turner, H., & Kracke, K. (2011). *The juvenile victimization took kit.* Retrieved from www.unh.edu/ccrc/jvq/available_versions.html

Hargreaves, A. (2000). Mixed emotions: Teachers' perceptions of their interactions with students. *Teaching and Teacher Education, 16,* 811–826. doi:10.1016/S0742-051X(00)00028-7

Harris, M., & Fallor, R. (2001). *Using trauma theory to design service systems: New directions for mental health services.* San Francisco, CA: Jossey-Bass.

Hastings, P. D., Zahn-Waxler, C., & McShane, K. (2006). We are, by nature, moral creatures: Biological bases of concern for others. In M. Killen, & J. G. Smetana (Eds.), *Handbook of moral development* (pp. 483–516). Mahwah, NJ: Erlbaum.

Hill, A. C. (2011). *The cost of caring: An investigation of the effects of teaching traumatized children in urban, elementary settings* (Doctoral dissertation, University of Massachusetts). Retrieved from http://scholarworks.umass.edu/cgi/viewcontent.cgi?article=1396&context=open_access_dissertations

Hughes, D. A., & Baylin, J. (2012). *Brain-based parenting: The neuroscience of caregiving for healthy attachment.* New York, NY: Norton.

Institute of Medicine of the National Academies. (2013). *New directions in child abuse and neglect.* Washington, DC: Author.

Jablow, P. (2014). Addressing childhood trauma in schools. *The Philadelphia Public School Notebook: Focus on Behavioral Health in Schools, 22*(3). Retrieved from http://thenotebook.org/december-2014/147967/addressing-childhood-trauma-schools-expert-views

Jagadeesan, L. M. (2012). *Attachment and social behavior in middle childhood: A comparison of maltreated and non-maltreated children.* Retrieved from University of Minnesota Digital Conservatory http://purl.umn.edu/137494

Jennings, P. A., & Greenberg, M. T. (2009). The prosocial classroom: Teacher social and emotional competence in relation to student and classroom outcomes. *Review of Educational Research, 79,* 491–525. doi:10.3102/0034654308325693

Jennings, P., Snowberg, K., Coccia, M., & Greenberg, M. (2011). Improving classroom learning environments by cultivating awareness and resilience in education: Results of two pilot studies. *Journal of Classroom Instruction, 46*(1), 37–48.

Jensen, E. (2008*). Brain-based learning: The new paradigm of teaching.* Thousand Oaks, CA: Corwin Press.

Jensen, E. (2013) *Engaging students with poverty in mind: Practical strategies for raising achievement.* Alexandria, VA: ASCD.

Johnson, S., Cooper, C., Cartwright, S., Donald, I., Taylor, P. J., & Millet, C. (2005). The experience of work related stress across occupations. *Journal of Managerial Psychology, 20*(2), 178–187. doi: 10.1108/02683940510579803

Johnson, D., & Johnson, D. (1985). *Cooperative learning: Warm ups, grouping strategies and group activities.* Edina, MN: Interaction Book Company.

Johnson, S. B., Riley, A. W., Granger, D. A., & Riis, J. (2013). The science of early life toxic stress for pediatric practice and advocacy. *Pediatrics, 131,* 319–327. doi:10.1542/peds.2012-0469

Johnson, S. M., Reinhorn, S. K., Charner-Laird, M., Kraft, M. A., Ng, M., & Papay, J. P. (2014). Ready to lead, but how? Teachers' experiences in high-poverty urban schools. *Teachers College Record, 116*(10), 1–50.

Johnston, P. H. (2012). *Opening minds: Using language to change lives.* Portland, ME: Stenhouse.

Jonson-Reid, M., Drake, B., Kim, J., Porterfield, S., & Han, L. (2004). A prospective analysis of the relationship between reported maltreatment and special education eligibility among poor children. *Child Maltreatment, 9*(4), 382–394.

Kagan, J. (2002). *Surprise, uncertainty and mental structures.* Cambridge, MA: Harvard University Press.

Kaiser Greenland, S. (2010). *The mindful child: How to help your kid manage stress and become happier, kinder, and more compassionate.* New York, NY: Free Press.

Karr-Morse, R., & Wiley, M. S. (2012). *Scared sick: The role of childhood trauma in adult disease.* Philadelphia, PA: Basic Books.

Kauffman, J. M., & Badar, J. (2013). How we might make special education for students with emotional or behavioral disorders less stigmatizing. *Behavioral Disorders, 39*, 16–27.

Klassen, R. M., Perry, N. E., & Frenzel, A. C. (2012). Teachers' relatedness with students: An underemphasized component of teachers' basic psychological needs. *Journal of Educational Psychology, 104*, 150–165. doi:10.1037/a0026253

Klusmann, U., Kunter, M., Trautwein, U., Ludtke, O., & Baumert, J. (2008). Teacher occupational well-being and quality of instruction: The important role of self-regulatory patterns. *Journal of Educational Psychology, 100*, 702–715. doi:10.1037/0022-0663.100.3.702

Lansford, J. E., Miller-Johnson, S., Berlin, L. J., Dodge, K. A., Bates, J. E., & Pettit, G. J. (2007). Early physical abuse and later violent delinquency: A prospective longitudinal study. *Child Maltreatment, 12*(3), 233–245.

Leahy, M. (2015). When experts miss trauma in children. *Psych Central.* Retrieved from http://psychcentral.com/lib/when-experts-miss-trauma-in-children/

Lee, C. D. (2007). *Culture, literacy, and learning: Taking bloom in the midst of the whirlwind.* New York, NY: Teachers College Press.

Lemov, D. (2010). *Teach like a champion: 49 techniques that put students on the path to college (K–12).* San Francisco, CA: Jossey-Bass.

Levine, M. D. (2002). *A mind at a time.* New York, NY: Simon & Schuster.

Levine, P., & Kline, M. (2006). Trauma through a child's eyes: Awakening the ordinary miracle of healing. Berkeley, CA: North Atlantic Books.

Lieberman, A., & Van Horn, P. (2013). Infants and young children in military families: A conceptual model for intervention. *Clinical Child and Family Psychology Review, 16*, 282–293. doi:10.1007/s10567-013-0140-4

Long, N. J., Fecser, F. A., & Brendtro, L. K. (1998). Life space crisis intervention: New skills for reclaiming students showing patterns of self-defeating behavior. *Healing Magazine, 3*(2), 2–23. Retrieved from http://www.lsci.org/files/lsci/professionals/LSCI-Article.pdf

Lovallo, W. R. (2005). *Stress & health: Biological and psychological interactions* (2nd ed.). Thousand Oaks, CA: Sage.

Luby, J., Belden, A., Botteron, K., Marrus, N., Harms, M., Babb, C., . . . Barch, D. (2013). The effects of poverty on childhood brain development: The mediating effect of caregiving and stressful life events. *JAMA Pediatrics, 167,* 1135–1142. doi:10.1001/jamapediatrics.2013.3139

Martin, H. (1979). Child abuse and development. *Child Abuse and Neglect, 3,* 415–421.

McCrory, E., De Brito, S., & Viding, E. (2011). The impact of childhood maltreatment: A review of neurological and genetic factors. *Frontiers in Psychiatry, 2*(48), 1–14. doi:10.3389/fpsyt.2011.00048

Mischel, W., Ebbesen, E. B., & Raskoff Zeiss, A. (1972). Cognitive and attentional mechanisms in delay of gratification. *Journal of Personality and Social Psychology, 21,* 204–218. doi:10.1037/h0032198

Money, J. (1982). Child abuse: Growth failure, I.Q. deficit, and learning disability, *Journal of Learning Disabilities, 120,* 439–446.

Mullinar, L., & Hunt, C. (Eds.) (1997). *Breaking the silence: Survivors of child abuse speak out.* Sydney, Australia: Hodder & Stoughton.

National Child Traumatic Stress Network. (2009). *Child traumatic stress introduction information sheets.* Retrieved from http://www.nctsn.org

National Child Traumatic Stress Network Schools Committee (2008). *Child trauma toolkit for educators.* Los Angeles, CA & Durham, NC: NCCTS.

National Commission on Teaching and America's Future. (2007). *The high cost of teacher turnover.* Washington, DC: Author.

National Scientific Center on the Developing Child (2005). *Excessive stress disrupts the architecture of the developing brain* (Working Paper No. 3). Retrieved from www.developingchild.harvard.edu/indez.php/resources/reports and working papers/working papers/wp3

National Scientific Center on the Developing Child (2006). *Early exposure to toxic substances damages brain architecture* (Working Paper No. 4). Retrieved from www.developingchild.harvard.edu/index.php/resources/reports/resources/reports and working papers/working papers/wp4

National Scientific Council on the Developing Child (2007). *The timing and quality of early life experiences combine to shape brain architecture* (Working Paper No. 5). Retrieved from http://developingchild.harvard.edu/index.php/resources/reports and working papers/working papers/wp5

National Scientific Council on the Developing Child. (2010). *Early experiences can alter gene expression and affect long-term development* (Working Paper No. 10). Retrieved from www.developingchild.harvard.edu

National Scientific Council on the Developing Child (2012). *The science of neglect: The persistent absence of responsive care disrupts the developing brain* (Working Paper No.12). Retrieved from developingchild.harvard.edu/index.php/resources/reports and working papers/working papers/wp12/

New America Foundation (2013). *Federal education budget.* Retrieved from www.newamerica.net/background

No Child Left Behind (NCLB) Act of 2001, Pub. L. No. 107-110, § 115, Stat. 1425 (2002).

Noguera, P. A. (1995). Preventing and producing violence: A critical analysis of responses to school violence. *Harvard Educational Review, 65,* 189–212.

Nystrand, M. (2006). Research on the role of classroom discourse as it affects reading comprehension. *Research in the Teaching of English, 40,* 393–412.

O'Connor, E., & McCartney, K. (2007). Examining teacher–child relationships and achievement as part of an ecological model of development. *American Educational Research Journal, 44*, 340–369. doi:10.3102/0002831207302172

Oehlberg, B. (2012). *Ending the shame: Transforming public education so it works for all students*. Pittsburgh, PA: RoseDog Books.

Osofsky, J. D. & Osofsky, H. J. (1999). Developmental implications of violence in youth. In M. Levine, W. B. Carey, & A. C. Crocker (Eds.), *Developmental and behavioral pediatrics* (3rd ed., pp. 493–498). Philadelphia, PA: W. B. Saunders.

Parker, P. D., & Martin, A. J. (2009). Coping and buoyancy in the work place : Understanding their effect on teachers' work related well-being and engagement. *Teaching and Teacher Education 25*(1), 68–75.

Peckham, H. (2013). Epigenetics: The dogma-defying discovery that genes learn from experience. *International Journal of Neuropsychotherapy, 1*, 9–20. doi:10.12744/ijnpt.2013.0009-0020

Perkins, M., & Graham-Bermann, S. (2012). Violence exposure and the development of school-related functioning: Mental health, neurocognition, and learning. *Aggression and Violent Behavior, 17*(1), 89–98.

Perry, B. (1997). Incubated in terror: Neurodevelopmental factors in the "cycle of violence." In J. Osofsky (Ed.), *Children in a violent society* (pp. 124–145). New York: Guilford Press.

Perry, B. (2002). Childhood experiences and the expression of genetic potential: What children can tell us about nature and nurture. *Brain and Mind, 3*, 79–100.

Perry, B. (2006). Applying principles of neurodevelopment to clinical work with maltreated and traumatized children: The neurosequential model of therapeutics. In N. B. Webb (Ed.), *Working with traumatized youth in child welfare* (pp. 27–52). New York, NY: Guilford Press.

Perry, B. (2013). *Bonding and attachment in maltreated children: Consequences of emotional neglect in childhood*. Houston, TX: The ChildTrauma Academy.

Perry, B. (2014). The cost of caring: Understanding and preventing secondary stress when working with traumatized and maltreated children. *CTA parent and caregiver education series 2*(7). Houston, TX: The ChildTrauma Academy Press.

Porche, M. V., Fortuna, L. R., Lin, J., & Alegria, M. (2011). Childhood trauma and psychiatric disorders as correlates of school dropout in a national sample of young adults. *Child Development, 82*(3), 982–998.

Portnoy, D. (2011). Burnout and compassion fatigue: Watch for the signs. *Health Progress 92*(4), 45–50. Retrieved from http://www.compassionfatigue.org/pages/healthprogress.pdf

Quinn, M., Rutherford, R. B., Leone, P. F. (2001). *Students with disabilities in correctional facilities*. Reston, VA: ERIC Clearing House on Disabilities and Gifted Education.

Rameson, L. T., & Lieberman, M. (2009). Empathy: A social cognitive neuroscience approach. *Social and Personality Psychology Compass, 3*, 94–110. doi:10.1111/j.1751-9004.2008.00154.x

Rapoport, J. L., & Gogtay, N. (2008). Brain neuroplasticity in healthy, hyperactive, and psychotic children: Insights from neuroimaging. *Neuropsychopharmacology, 33*, 181–197. doi:10.1038/sj.npp.1301553

Roeser, R. W., Skinner, E., Beers, J., & Jennings, P. (2012). Mindfulness training and teachers' professional development. *Child Developmental Perspectives 6*(2), 167–173. doi:10 1111/j.1750-8606.2012.000238

Ronfeldt, M., Loeb, S., & Wyckoff, J. (2013, February). How teacher turnover harms student achievement. *American Educational Research Journal, 50,* 4–36. doi:10.3102/0002831212463813

Rosenbloom, D. J., Pratt, A. C., & Pearlman, L. A. (1995). Helpers' responses to trauma work: Understanding and intervening in an organization. In B. H. Stamm (Ed.), *Secondary traumatic stress: Self-care issues for clinicians, researchers, and educators* (pp. 65–79). Baltimore, MD: Sidran Press.

Rosenfeld, L. R., Richman, J. M., & Bowen, C. L. (2000). Social support networks and school outcomes: The centrality of the teacher. *Child and Adolescent Social Work Journal, 17,* 205–226. doi:10.1023/A%3A1007535930286

Rude, S. S., Wenglaff, R. M., Gibbs, B., Vane, J., & Whitney, T. (2002). Negativity biases predict subsequent depressive symptoms. *Cognition and Emotion, 16*(3), 423–440.

Schore, A. N. (2001). Effects of a secure attachment relationship on right brain development, affect regulation, and infant mental health. *Infant Mental Health Journal, 22,* 7–66. doi:10.1002/1097-0355(200101/04)22:1<7::AID-IMHJ2>3.0.CO;2-N

Schore, A. N. (2003). Early relational trauma, disorganized attachment, and the development of a predisposition to violence. In M. Solomon, & D. Siegel (Eds.), *Healing trauma: Attachment, mind, body and brain* (pp. 107–167). New York, NY: Norton.

Schore, J., & Schore, A. N. (2008). Modern attachment theory: The central role of affect regulation in development and treatment. *Clinical Social Work Journal, 36,* 9–20. doi:10.1007/s10615-007-0111-7

Schuengel, C., Oosterman, M., & Sterkenburg, P. S. (2009). Children with disrupted attachment histories: Interventions and psychophysiological indices of effects. *Child and Adolescent Psychiatry and Mental Health, 26.* doi:10.1186/1753-2000-3-26

Shonkoff, J. P., & Garner, A. S. (2012). The lifelong effects of early childhood adversity and toxic stress. *Pediatrics, 129,* e232–e246. doi:10.1542/peds.2011-2663

Siegel, D. J. (2010). *Mindsight: The new science of personal transformation.* New York, NY: Bantam Books.

Siegel, D. J. (2012). *The developing mind: How relationships and the brain interact to shape who we are* (2nd ed.). New York, NY: Guilford Press.

Siegel, D. J., & Bryson, T. P. (2012). *The whole-brain child: 12 revolutionary strategies to nurture your child's developing mind.* New York, NY: Bantam.

Siegel, D. J., & Bryson, T. P. (2014). No-drama discipline: The whole-brain way to calm the chaos and nurture your child's developing mind. New York, NY: Bantam.

Siegler, R.S. (1998) *Children's thinking.* Upper Saddle River, NJ: Prentice-Hall.

Sigelman, C. K., & Rider, E. A. (2015). *Life-span human development* (8th ed.). Stamford, CT: Cengage Learning.

Simon, S. N., & Johnson, S. M. (2015). Teacher turnover in high-poverty schools: What we know and can do. *Teachers College Record, 117*(3), 1–36.

Skinner, E., & Beers, J. (in press). Mindfulness and teachers' coping in the classroom: A developmental model of teacher stress, coping, and everyday resilience. In K. Schonert-Reichl, & R. W. Roeser (Eds.), *Handbook on mindfulness in education: Emerging theory, research, and programs.* New York, NY: Springer-Verlag.

Snyder, H. N. (2005). *Juvenile arrests 2003. OJJDP Juvenile Justice Bulletin*, p. 9. Washington, DC: Office of Juvenile Justice and Delinquency Prevention, Office of Justice Programs, U.S. Department of Justice.

Spillane, J. P., Hallett, T., & Diamond, J. B. (2003). Forms of capital and the construction of leadership: Instructional leadership in urban elementary schools. *Sociology of Education, 76*, 1–17.

Sprague, J. (2014). Integrating PBIS and Restorative Discipline. *The Special EDge, 27*(3), 11–13. Retrieved from www.calstat.org/publications/article_detail.php?a_id=215&nl_id=130

Sprenger, M. (2013). *Teaching the critical vocabulary of the common core: 55 words that make or break student understanding*. Alexandria, VA: ASCD.

Sugai, G., Horner, R. H., Dunlap, G., Hieneman, M., Lewis, T. J., Nelson, C. M., . . . Ruef, M. B. (2000). Applying positive behavior support and functional behavioral assessment in schools. *Journal of Positive Behavior Interventions, 2*, 131–143. doi:10.1177/109830070000200302

Taylor, D. (2013, June 10). Link between early trauma and bad health. *Philadelphia Inquirer.* Retrieved from articles.philly.com/2013-06-10/news/39875238_1_aces-heart-disease-infectious-disease

Teicher, M. H. (2000). Wounds that time won't heal. *Cerebrum.* Retrieved from www.dana.org/Cerebrum/2000/Wounds_That_Time_won't_Heal_The_Neurobiology_of_Child_Abuse.

Teicher, M. H., Anderson, C. M., & Polcari, A. (2012). Childhood maltreatment is associated with reduced volume in hippocampus subfields CA3, denate gyrus and subiculum. *Proceedings of the National Academy of Sciences of USA, 109*(9), E563–E572.

Teicher, M. H., Anderson, S. L., Polcari, A., Anderson, C. M., & Navalta, C. P. (2002). Developmental neurobiology of childhood stress and trauma. *The Psychiatric Clinics of North America, 25*, 397–426. doi:10.1016/S0193-953X(01)00003-X

Teicher, M. H., Dumont, N. L., Ito, Y., Vaituzis, C., Giedd, J. N., & Andersen, S. L. (2004). Childhood neglect is associated with reduced corpus callosum area. *Biological Psychiatry, 56*, 80–85. doi:10.1016/j.biopsych.2004.03.016

Tomlinson, C. A. (2001). *How to differentiate instruction in mixed-ability classrooms* (2nd ed.). Alexandria, VA: Association for Supervision and Curriculum Development.

Tucker, D. M. (1992). Developing emotions and cortical networks. In M. R. Gunner, & C. A. Nelson (Eds.), *Developmental behavioral neuroscience: The Minnesota symposia on child psychology* (vol. 24, pp. 75–128). Hillsdale, NJ: Lawrence Erlbaum

Tugade, M. M., Frederickson, B. L. & Barrett, L. F. (2004). Psychological resilience and positive emotional granularity: Examining the benefits of positive emotion on coping and health. *Journal of Personality 72*(6), 1161–1190. doi:10.1111/I 1467-6494-2004-00294.x

van der Kolk, B. (2001). *Remarks at Helping Traumatized Children Learn conference* [Transcript on file at Massachusetts Advocates for Children, 25 Kingston Street, Boston, MA 02111, 617-357-8436]. Paper presented at the Lesley College, Massachusetts Advocates for Children (MAC), and the Task Force on Children Affected by Domestic Violence, Cambridge, MA.

van der Kolk, B. A. (2003). The neurobiology of childhood trauma and abuse. *Child Adolescent Psychiatric Clinics of North America, 12*(2), 293–317.

van der Kolk, B. A. (2005). Developmental trauma disorder. *Psychiatric Annals, 35*, 401–408. Retrieved from http://www.wjcia.org/conpast/2008/trauma/trauma.pdf

van der Kolk, B. A. (2008). Developmental trauma disorder:Toward a rational diagnosis of children with complex trauma histories. *Praxis der kinderpsychologie und kinderpsychiatrie, 58*(8), 572–586. Translation retrieved at www.trauma-center.org/products/pdf_file/preprint_dev_trauma_disorder.pdf

van der Kolk, B. (2014). *The body keeps the score: Brain, mind, and body in the healing of trauma.* New York, NY: Viking.

Warren, M. R. (2005). Communities and schools: A new view of urban education reform. *Harvard Educational Review, 75*, 133–173. Retrieved from isites.harvard.edu/fs/docs/icb.topic1373484.files/Warren_2005.pdf

Wiley, M. S. (2004). The limits of talk: An interview with Bessel van der Kolk. *Psychotherapy Networker, 28*(4), 1–5.

Wilson, J. Q., & Kelling, G. L. (1982, March 1). Broken windows: The police and neighborhood safety. *The Atlantic, 249*, 29–38. Retrieved from www.theatlantic.com/magazine/archive/1982/03/broken-windows/304465/

Willis, J.A.(2008). Building a bridge from neuroscience to the classroom. *Phi Delta Kappan. 89*(6), 424–427.

Wolpow, R., Johnson, M. M., Hertel, R., & Kincaid, S. O. (2009). *The heart of learning and teaching: Compassion, resiliency, and academic success.* State of Washington Office of Superintendent of Public Instruction. Retrieved from http://www.k12.wa.us/compassionateschools/pubdocs/theheartoflearningandteaching.pdf

Zapf, D. (2002). Emotion work and psychological well-being: A review of the literature and some conceptual considerations. *Human Resource Management Review, 12*, 237–268. doi:10.1016/S1053-4822(02)00048-7

Zhao, Y. (2014). *Who's afraid of the big, bad dragon? Why China has the best (and the worst) education system in the world.* San Francisco, CA: Jossey-Bass.

Index

About the Author

Susan E. Craig, PhD, completed her doctorate in sociology at the University of New Hampshire and a postdoctoral fellowship at the University of Miami. She is a lifelong student of early trauma and its effects on children's learning. Her teaching experience, as well as years of on-site training and technical assistance to school districts throughout the country, provides the context for her advocacy for trauma-sensitive educational reform.

Dr. Craig began her writing career in 1992 with an article in *Phi Delta Kappan* describing the educational needs of children living with violence. This work received special notice in the now famous "purple book" *Helping Traumatized Children Learn* (2005) published by Massachusetts Advocates for Children: Trauma and Policy Initiative. Her book *Reaching and Teaching Children Who Hurt: Strategies for Your Classroom* (2008) is a bestseller among teachers and administrators, who use it to guide their efforts to make schools more accessible to children with challenging behaviors. In 2013, Dr. Craig was among those interviewed in the Safe Start National Resource Center series profiling women who have made an impact on the issue of children's exposure to violence.

Dr. Craig is an avid blogger and sought-after public speaker. Her blog, www.meltdownstomastery.wordpress.com, covers topics of interest to educators working with traumatized children.